Meeting My Angel

Michelle Shippel

Published by TW Publishers
E-mail: hello@twpublishers.co.za
Website: www.twpublishers.co.za
Office: +27647794326 / WhatsApp: +27647794326
47 Thomas Street, Olifantsfontein
Midrand, South Africa

Disclaimer: The purpose of this book is to educate and entertain. The author and/or publisher do not guarantee that anyone following these techniques, suggestions, tips, ideas, or strategies will become successful. The author and/or publisher shall have neither liability nor responsibility to anyone with respect to any loss or damage caused, or alleged to be caused, directly or indirectly by the information contained in this book.

Typeset in Stix Two Text, 12pts
ISBN: 978-1-990968-48-8

Dedication

I would like to dedicate this book to those who have stood by me throughout my fertility and adoption journey. I cannot fully express how much you all mean to me and how you have helped me achieve my dream. Thank you from the bottom of my heart.

Dr G, you are truly one in a million! My other father! Thank you for never giving up on me and my dreams! You and your amazing team hold a very special place in my heart and you always will. I am so thankful we had the time to get to know one another and I will treasure each moment we got to bond. Your constant encouragement and unwavering support meant so much to me. More than you could possibly know!

To our second family Vitalab, your warmth, love, kindness and constant encouragement will never be forgotten. It is never easy doing the work you do on a daily basis. However, we were always greeted with smiles, laughter and love. You made a downright uncomfortable and shitty process easier to deal with and accept. I treasure all the chats and laughter we shared. Thank you!

Tanya, your constant guidance, love, support and counseling are deeply appreciated! In your own subtle and gentle way what you have done for us and still do for us on a daily basis is absolutely remarkable. You have always been there for me and us and to this day you never cease to amaze me. Thank you! You are so appreciated and loved and I would not have gotten to this point without you.

To the lady who made it all happen. Zoe, there are absolutely no words that suffice in thanking you for what you have done for us. We are so grateful for having you in our lives and treasure every day that we know you. You have given us our greatest gift and have been there for us every step of the way. Your guidance, support, knowledge, love and passion for what you do is a true reflection of who you are. We are thankful for having you in our lives and wish you and your loved ones a life full of its richest blessings.

Bubs, you have been by my side right through our journey and you have supported and loved me unconditionally throughout our relationship. I love you dearly and am so thankful that you are part of my life and my story. Without you there is nothing to live for and fight for. My rock, my partner, my other half.

Thank you! I love you!

Raphy my love, you are mommy's Angel! Thank you for choosing me to be yours. It is an honour for me to be your mommy. I love you endlessly and I am so proud of you my Spoonk! You mean the world to daddy and me and we treasure you eternally. My human Angel, you are everything to me and more. Thank you for being in my life Raphaely! May everyone know just how special you are and how grateful we are that we belong to each other. Mommy and Daddy love you eternally, sweet boy!

Contents

Meeting My Angel

You never know what challenges others are going through – so just be nice!

Foreword

"This is a most revealing and intimate true life story which we are about to have the privilege to witness.

This profound account reveals the infertility journey - the highs and the lows, the disappointments, the hopes and sorrows. It shows how the final painful decision to achieve closure is reached.

A new journey begins - adoption - providing new challenges, hope, excitement and new reachable goals! Then the home-run where a dim light at the end of a long tunnel is a goal.

As the journey progresses the light at the end of the tunnel brightens. Finally a match made in heaven is suddenly real and attainable. A cherub is born and finds his forever family who brightens his world forever ."

Zoe Cohen
Adoption Councilor

The end is really just the beginning! This story is as hopeful as it is heartbreaking!

For many of us we expect our life to go according to plan, once we have found our partner, we will marry, have children and fulfill all of our life's plans and dreams! But what happens when those expectations that we have created are turned upside down!

The infertility journey as we call it, can only be described as one of the most difficult journeys in life. A journey that unravels and challenges us on every possible level. Financially the challenges are enormous. Physically although you do what you have to do to get through it, each injection, each scan, and each blood test. The hardest part often for many patients is the emotional and spiritual impact of the journey. There is nothing like infertility to unravel you as a person. Emotional pain is so much greater than the physical pain. The physical pain disappears eventually but the emotional longing for a child, that endless hope, desire, wish, want and intangible dream lasts forever! The hope with each month and each treatment that this was THE one, coupled with the absolute devastation that this in fact wasn't the one!

Hope is the cruelest of them all because it holds your hand each time, but it lets you down each time too. Its empty promises keep you going time and time again. And why shouldn't they, it's only the hope that this cycle might be THE cycle that works. That this method might be THE method that works. It breaks you down into a million pieces, time and time again and somehow inadvertently builds you up time and time again and keeps you going. The irony is that without the hope, we wouldn't be able to pick ourselves up and try again.

I have been privileged to work with countless couples navigating this journey and the intimate balance of hope and fear, uncertainty and grief. It has been an honor to watch Michelle and Jared's story unfold and hold this sacred space for them. This story shows us how resilient this couple is and how as human beings you are able to go through unimaginable pain yet at the same time have the capacity to endure and thrive and somehow come out the other side. This book is a book of courage, strength, determination and most of all, a gift of truly meeting an angel.

Tanya Rubin

Michelle and Jared have travelled a long path throughout their journey as a couple, which unfortunately resulted in a diagnosis of infertility. After many assisted reproduction technology treatments, and empty, broken promises of conception, they have had a child of their own.

I am often asked how many couples I can really help to achieve their dream of taking home a baby, and my answer is always that it depends on what measures the couple would be willing to go to.

Being the couple's physician, it was an honor and privilege to watch Michelle and Jared enter their own brave, new world, and follow their passage of becoming parents via the process of adoption.

I trust that this book will be of value to many couples who will need to consider the path of adoption. Thank you, Michelle, Jared, and Raphi, for your contribution to our ever-increasing problem of infertility management.

Lawrence Gobetz, Medical Director, Vitalab

The Beginning!

Hi! My name is Michelle and this is my true account of my infertility journey.

Hectic yes, full of love, definitely. Anger - oh for sure - and kids? We will see... Sit back, get comfy and I really hope you enjoy.

When I was roughly 22 years old, I was told that I have Mosaic Turners Syndrome. For all intents and purposes, I am a very healthy 34 year old. However, the way that the syndrome showed up in me if you look closely is shorter limbs, wider chest, which I can pass off as a swimmer and unfortunately I am unable to have children. My ovaries are quite small and I do not have my own eggs. The technical term would be peri-menopausal. I also have a hemi-uterus – my uterus is a little squiff and before I was operated on, I had limited space inside my uterus to even consider carrying a fetus. Initially, my knowledge of the syndrome was pretty limited. I was filled with anger and I had an undeniable hatred for doctors, even those I did not know.

So, while we were still in the dating phase of our relationship, one evening I decided that it was time to explain to my husband what it really meant to be in a relationship with me and obviously a view to marrying me. I knew that this was the man I wanted to be with for the rest of my life and although I was not sure of what his response would be, I knew that I just had to take the chance and jump in and tell him. I felt that I really owed it to him and I did not want to keep this a secret any longer. This was a huge step for me! From the moment I was told about my situation I felt like a complete alien, I felt like I just did not belong anywhere and although before this I knew somehow I was different and I did not fit in with the crowd, I felt it even more now. It was completely uncomfortable. I was unhappy and I trusted no one! I was lucky enough to even have met and accepted going for coffee with my other half because although I trusted myself I did not trust people and did not believe in good intent. Pretty damaging hey! Now, you will certainly ask me why it is that I do not trust people. If I look back to when I was a child, my life was consumed with endless doctor visits, pain and operations. Trauma. It was not for the faint of heart and I had no idea how to deal with any of my emotions.

Of course, parents being parents, mine weren't sure it was a good idea for me to be saying anything to Jared. I could not have been more sure and I did it anyway and I am so glad that I did. Turns out, he knew the doctor I was meant to meet with and he knew more about my condition than I did. He studied it in genetics at university. I explained the situation and of course being the person that I am, I said to him that I completely understand if he wants to leave and would rather not be in a relationship with me. Funnily enough he was apparently quite offended and refused to go anywhere and thankfully we are married now just over 10 years and together for 12 and a half amazing years.

When the proposal came, I was right in the middle of my English Honors year. The year was particularly difficult on me and when my other half proposed, it was really like a breath of fresh air. It was exactly what I needed as it gave me something amazing to look forward to. However, infinitely more stress. I now had to plan for a wedding. My wedding! Shit! I was getting married! I actually said yes!? Ok, battle stations everyone, we are in for a bumpy ride. So, while completing my stressful and hectic honours year, I was organizing stuff for the wedding ....

PS: My husband has written his experiences and thoughts on this as well, our writings are separated by the lovely icon below.

Mich has summed up the beginning of our journey pretty concisely. As you can see she was very open with me about what I was getting myself into but that didn't deter me at all. I knew long before she told me that this was my future wife and it would take an absolutely cataclysmic issue to get me to change my mind. We were tested to our limits but this journey has taught us so much about ourselves, each other, life and unconditional love.

Thank you so much for sharing our journey with us!

Meeting My Angel

You never know what challenges others are going through – so just be nice!

And So It Goes

Our special day!

My other half has just stepped on the glass! The ring has been placed on my finger. We are finally married! What a beautiful and amazing ceremony. I really felt so accepted, loved and I even managed to get the photographer to get a shot of us holding hands under the Chuppah. I just thought it was a really memorable shot and summed our relationship up beautifully – always hand in hand, together, strong, united. We were given a bit of time together as a newly married couple, then photos were taken as usual, with family and alone and then the party began. What a night!

I was so overwhelmed and excited that when I woke up the next morning in the hotel, I took one look at my finger with the newly placed wedding band and thought, "oh my gosh! What on earth have I just done?" I calmed down a little while later when I realized that we still had to open our presents.

We spent the next three months floating between both sets of parents, while juggling work, organizing our new home, spending time together as a newly married couple and so much more. Finally, it came time to move into our place. Of course any couple would at this point think happily every after. Nope! We were in for massive challenges, changes, honesty, closeness and eventually something we may or may not have been ready for – fertility treatment – a lot of it!

As the year continued and we began to settle further into a normal routine and married life, I began waking up exhausted. Why? I did not consciously know. All I knew was that maybe I needed to be checked by the doctor because there was a possible deficiency of some sort. So, a trip to the GP was the first step in our story. I was examined and told that maybe I needed to get in touch with a geneticist and there and then it was suggested that we make an appointment to meet with Dr Gobetz. The GP thought that I could possibly, subconsciously, be thinking about my condition, wanting to explore more and of course maybe felt it was time to start planning our family. Wow! so much to take in! But why did I need to see a geneticist? What was going on with me?

The date to meet at the Donald Gordon arrived. Full of nerves and unsure of what to expect from the consultation, we began by explaining what brought us through to Professor X, as in from the X-Men - yes another reference to me being "different". Rather this time I preferred to think of myself as having super powers. I haven't quite thought of what those might be though but I humored myself anyway (Jared says I am gifted with an innate bullshit detector, a capacity to love unconditionally and my Kryptonite – impatience which is held at bay by the odd swear word. The more impatient I get, the more I swear).

Professor X was a really lovely and down to earth lady who managed to put everything into perspective and direct us accordingly. I was examined yet again and a date for a follow up session was given to us. In the meanwhile, I remembered that my previous GP had all of my medical records stored away and surely there must have been something of value there as he was around throughout my childhood, although mentioned nothing to me about my condition at all. Strange! What a Poes though! (And I used the capital "P" on purpose!) I called the secretary and told her to have my records ready and waiting for me as I was coming to collect. I arrived and not one sheet of paper was ready and waiting for me. Of course this pissed me off hugely and I personally went into his drawer, pulled out all of my medical records, while being gawked at by a full waiting room as well as two very incompetent and stupid secretaries if you wish to call them that even. As I marched right out of the rooms, with all this information, the waiting room filled with people, just watched in amazement and the two ladies just giggled and thought I was being unreasonable and would probably return at some point. Gladly I have never returned following that incident and I never even received a call as to why I behaved in the manner that I did. He obviously knew that he should have done more to assist me and to be more supportive. I have not for one moment looked back. Good riddance to filth!

The day had arrived for us to meet with Dr G. I was really confused emotionally and just putting myself in this situation was immensely tough for me. On entering through Vitalab's doors for the very first time, I had never before felt such acceptance, warmth and love from a doctor or his team. It was a very unsettling feeling for me. As Lawrence saw us, he greeted my other half, asked how the family was and then Dr G. introduced himself to me and shook my hand. I responded accordingly and mentioned to him that he probably knows me by my maiden name. After thinking for a second, he said "I was waiting for you! I knew this skeleton was going to come out of the closet at some point." Apparently there was a file already opened regarding my case. So just to put you in the picture, my parents had met him when I was a young teen and he wanted me to come through to meet with him so that he could explain everything to me properly. My parents decided it was not the right time for this and rather I should focus on my studies and complete my matric without concerning myself with those sorts of things. Hindsight is always 20/20.

There was so much anger that fuelled this first meeting! We all know that when you are prepared for a fight it is not easy going into a conversation with a clear and open mind.

We were then directed to a small, darkened, scanning room. I did not know what to expect. I was told to remove pants, shoes and underwear, climb on the bed and cover up with a blanket. Within a few moments,

Dr G walked in and like a wizard who draws his wand to perform magic tricks, he pulled out a long penis-like gadget, applied a condom onto it with gel and lo and behold, this was my very first internal examination with this scanning instrument. It was certainly void of magic. It was so weird! I had this deafening pounding in my chest. You could see everything from angles to size to different organs. It was really quite scary how advanced this equipment was and what it could tell you. Already, I was feeling quite terrified as he showed me, while being scanned, that my one ovary is considerably smaller than the other. It was almost as if one side of my uterus did not develop and hence we termed it a hemi-uterus. I just remember it being too much for me and on hearing this, I pushed forward and was about to get off the plinth, when Doctor G pushed me back and continued with the examination as if nothing happened.

Following my very interesting, daunting and invasive internal examination, we headed back to Dr. G's office and had a consultation. I sort of understood everything that Lawrence told us. However, it was a massive amount for me personally to process. We were drawn a diagram of my fucked up anatomy and explained the fertility and IVF process now and what needed to happen to try and get us pregnant. Costing was discussed and of course by the end of the consult I left even more angry, alone and misunderstood. Or so I thought. I was sent downstairs in the same building to have my blood taken and we were then allowed to leave.

It took a few days before we got the call for any of my blood results. At this point, Jared and I felt that maybe it was a good idea to try going for couples counseling. We wanted to have a more connected relationship and I felt that Jared needed help in trying to understand me a little better. We had just arrived at this lay counselor and stopped the car when we got the call from Dr G. He explained that technically I was peri-menopausal. Basically this meant that I was not ovulating like other women every month. We would have to go through with IVF using donor eggs as we did not know if the quality of my eggs if produced, were even of a decent quality.

I wanted to be "normal" like others who were able to fall pregnant naturally, carry their own babies to term and give birth naturally or through C-section. After our consult with Dr. G I remember sitting outside at our place on the porch and explaining that going through with the IVF treatment, the way it was planned for us, was not something I was happy with. We would have to use and insert someone else's eggs and I felt like this was one partner cheating on the other. I felt detached from the world and Jared. Unfortunately, I also felt worthless, completely useless and having my own children was really important to me. Of course, I was not thinking about that at the time. I was focused on the fact that this was all happening to me. I was being poked and prodded and examined and everything that had happened in my past with doctors, whether good or bad, had now resurfaced and I was not handling it very well at all!

I needed someone to hold my hand through all of this.

Everything was picture perfect at our wedding and we have always been exceptionally close. From a guy's perspective, many of you will not want to hear the "flowery" side of the beginning of our married life, but in order to understand my reactions to what was to come, I will offer a little bit of context from time to time.

The first thing you need to know about my life is that I had two amazing parents who loved each other more than life itself and were very rarely apart. Even when they had a fight, which was not all that common, it would be sorted out with compassion, communication and humor. We were always a very tight and close family and it was nothing to be ashamed of to talk about your feelings and show them too. The old adage of boys don't cry was never something that was imposed on me because you were simply not being true to yourself if you hid your emotions. Remember this! Showing your emotions and expressing your feelings helps immensely – and the road ahead is filled with so many ups and downs that not doing so can end up in you seeming unsupportive, cold or distant when your wife or partner needs you the most!

I was under no illusions that we would have our challenges with Mich's genetics. I did, however, want us to find out just how this had an impact on her physiologically. Thank G-d her heart and vital organs were very healthy. The obvious physical differences were something we could joke about. Her ability to have children was something we desperately hoped would be possible. And that is the second thing about me that has shaped my actions and responses throughout our journey – I look for the positive wherever I can; I believe that without hope in its basest form we can very easily slip into despair, anger and depression. I have always known that the odds were not with us but the alternative to believing that our journey would end as we envisioned was unthinkable. Some might say that I am obstinate and unrealistic, but this is how I have personally managed to cope while doing whatever I could to support my amazing wife who is my hero. I am so lucky to be her partner – in crime, in love, in sadness and in joy!

Meeting My Angel

You never know what challenges others are going through – so just be nice!

Desperate Times Call For Desperate Measures!

Once everything had calmed down on the genetics and fertility side, there was one more area that we had to explore. We had to rule out any dangers involved in me falling pregnant – as well as taking a closer look at my general health. I had to see a cardiologist. Apparently with this sort of medical condition, it is likely that there are possible heart defects. Worry, who me?!?! Of course I overthink and it takes me back to the few times that I have literally passed out getting out of a hot shower. It really is not fun. I now make sure I keep some sweets next to my bed so that I do not faint again – too late.

So, we made an appointment with the doctor and I was checked really thoroughly by such an amazing man. Of course, I was nervous but thankfully I was apparently in good health. I was given the "all clear" and was told I could go about my merry way.

The next four years were filled with ups and downs and some times were far more difficult than others. Of course we had been trying now for a while and we knew of the prognosis – we knew we needed help. It took me four long years to pull myself together and sort myself out on my own and realize that the house is just far to quiet for me. I needed to make something happen. I had been giving a lot of love and time to my other half and I really wanted to be able to expand this little family and share my love with another little being. No not my doggies! of course my doggies are very important to me and I love them very much, but I honestly felt that it was time to get results and soon. We were not getting younger and although at times I goof off and act like a big kid – probably from my drama background – I wanted a little person to be able to do it with. The house is lonely and all I wanted was to hear a little one laughing. My little one laughing. Now all I had in mind was a goal and that I needed to get there and that I would. I would achieve my goal of carrying my own child. I would do it! Or so I thought!

We tried and tried and tried some more. No one was any the wiser. All they saw was this girl who has a crass mouth and made inappropriate comments at times. Little did they know what was truly happening in the background. This reminds me of a situation I once found myself in.

My husband, my mom and I were sitting and having coffee. We saw an "interfering" woman that Jared and I know and she thought she could actually tell me that it was now time to give my in-laws grandchildren. Of course, I didn't take too kindly to her barking orders at me like a Chihuahua. She also thought it was her right to tell me that I should tell Jared to stop drinking milkshakes and that I should get an appointment with her reflexologist because she was the best. All would be right in the world and "Poof!!!", just like that I would fall pregnant. What utter tripe!!! Have you ever heard anything so stupid in your life?

But wait there's more! Somehow, she managed to get my phone number and as I was on my way home one afternoon from a client, I got a call that she was with her reflexologist and would like to make me an appointment. She immediately knew I was not happy to hear from her. Clever lady! You managed to understand the tone of my voice. I wished she would have followed through with backing off without me having to tell her because now she was upset with me for telling her that this is not the path that we are wanting to follow. My mom-in-law, who is really non-confrontational, very nicely had to tell her to let us be and that children was our business.

I wish with every part of my being that this person was right in her approach. I wish it was so easy falling pregnant. Unfortunately, these days it is becoming more and more difficult for people to fall pregnant and it is extremely expensive to have treatment.

Thankfully, there are special organizations out there that believe in this and are willing to help even if, in the end, it just doesn't happen. These people and organizations are so special that if it does not happen for you they will do whatever they can to make it happen and help you through the trauma and hell.

So, four years after all the doctor consults and testing, I plucked up the courage to return for another major shot at Vitalab. I had enough of waiting and wasting time. Jared got hold of Dr G and organized the appointment and within two weeks that seemed like an arduous eternity we were sitting again in the waiting room. All I saw was the different faces of nervous people who had no clue of where to put themselves or what to do or say. You see, you sit there with your partner and now, more often than not, you will see someone you know and the anxiety intensifies as you really don't want anyone else knowing about your "double life" as an infertile. Everything is cloak and dagger!

I had no clue of this when we started on this long journey until we awkwardly bumped into a couple we know and asked them to not say anything about our chance meeting. After all the years we spent at Vitalab making friends, meeting couples, helping people along the way, we eventually realized that we bump in to people we know and it is alright and that we are certainly not alone in this process. This was incredibly liberating! You think you are alone but you are never alone. No matter how dark, lonely, upsetting and terrifying the journey may be, you are never ever alone in the process. Unfortunately or fortunately, there is always me who has been through most of it.

I sat in the waiting room thinking about what we could expect, questions I might have, or anything else and in the next moment we were called into Dr G's office. As usual so kind and friendly and warm, he turns to Jared and asks how his family is doing and to me he warmly smiled and said lets get you pregnant. We were directed to the scanning room once again – this was to be a safe space for me from now until we said our goodbyes four years later. Little did I know that these "intimate" rooms were to be a safe haven for me eventually to be filled with many different emotions, swear words and of course those times where I was bursting to "take a pish" so badly! In order to make sure that I was given every opportunity of falling pregnant, I had to have medication injected into my uterus to aid in implantation and strengthening the womb.

We were told about the treatment plan that I would have to go on. We had a plan! We decided to do a mock cycle first to make sure we were on the right track and thankfully the medication worked well. We then had to step across to Veda, which is the egg donation wing of Vitalab. We sat with their in-house counselor who went through our requirements, asked a few questions and started emailing profiles through for us to look at of possible egg donors.

After analyzing each and every donor from their looks to eating habits; preferences to family history, we chose a profile – only to find out that she did not pitch. The counselor was really apologetic and all I could say was that this was obviously not the right donor for us and it was fine.

We picked another donor, after much the same ritual, and this went really well! I recall getting the call on the day that they performed her egg retrieval. I was so happy that I actually was crying a little. Wow! First sign of me being a bit more human or was it the pharmacy I was taking? I think the latter was the more appropriate answer. The day eventually came for the eggs to be fertilized and grow. We started with nineteen amazingly beautiful eggs, which whittled down to an outstanding eleven fertilized eggs and 8 embryos! The nursing staff were overjoyed. My husband was very happy. I was happy, although I did not know what the usual amount was. Once I found out that the number of eggs that we just ended up with was a really high one, I felt that we actually may just have a chance here.

Remember the hope I told you about before. Now more than ever it gave both of us a feeling that we could do this and leave the care of the doctors, nurses and amazing support staff at Vitalab with a child of our own. We needed help but in our minds there was never any question that Dr G and his unbelievable team, that were to become our second family, were going to help us get there. We just needed to be patient, try to let the process unfold and ignore those callous, barking "Chihuahuas" who felt that they knew what was best for us.

We were not going to try anything that didn't resonate with us or have ourselves ordered around by people who had absolutely no clue of what we were embarking on and had been experiencing in the first half decade of our married life. We were putting our faith in Dr G with G-d's help. And we were going to do this privately.

This meant we had to get our story straight between ourselves to answer any prying questions that might arise, and boy were we asked so many times when the babies were coming. We must have been fairly good at it because the people who didn't really know us seemed to accept our reasons; little white lies that were sparing our feelings and hiding our disappointment. How could they know that their "intrusive" questioning was at times hurtful and made the obvious so much more obvious. How could they realize the care we were taking in picking just the right egg donor and how much we wanted to believe that after that first IVF we would get the incredible news that we were expecting. How could they know that they were just making us more anxious and making me think about what could go wrong, what could go right and a million other "what ifs".

The one constant in my mind was that I was going to, and had to, be with Mich every step of the way. If we could not have a baby naturally together, we would still have one "unnaturally" but it would be together.

Meeting My Angel

You never know what challenges others are going through – so just be nice!

IVF: Take 1

That harrowing day for the IVF implant to be done had arrived quicker than I would have liked. What a day! The morning was hectic. I decided to work from home so no one knew what was going on. We pulled ourselves together and off we went. Once we arrived at "headquarters", we were directed to the IVF lab on the first floor. This was all very new for me. We were welcomed and made ourselves comfortable on lazy boys, while we filled out forms and I had my vitals checked. Of course they reiterated that I had to make sure to drink plenty of water and so I did! Once I enthusiastically polished off a one and a half litre bottle of Valpre water, I asked if I could go to the bathroom, obviously not realizing how close we were to having the transfer done. I was told I could only empty half the bladder. Can you explain to me exactly how does one do this? I don't know about you but half a piss just does not do it for me.

Finally, we were called in to theatre. It was an empty room with a bed or plinth-like thingy and computer screens. I was "kakking" myself. "Just breathe! Relax and it will all be over very soon." This is what I kept telling myself. Jared seemed excited, a little nervous, but of course, calm as always. I jumped up onto the bed in my gorgeous theatre overalls! They really did wonders for my eyes! The nurse and one of the doctors responsible for performing my transfer, then hastily strapped my legs up to the stirrups and I was now completely exposed, vulnerable. "Are they going to hurt me? What are they doing? Why strap me up? Is this a new form of S and M? I am completely freaking out here and no-one even knows! I don't think I want to do this anymore. I am scared! The pressure on the bladder, the pushing, prodding, having another man looking at my privates, how could I do this to my husband? Yes it is a medical thing but it still feels very strange and completely uncomfortable."

It was a resounding agreement that we implant one egg. Of course, I know that the chance of falling pregnant with putting one back is lower than if you had two but whatever happens happens, right? Wrong! After an awkward "feel up", I was done and we walked out and went home. The deed, which was meant to be meaningful and filled with love and excitement of what was hopefully to come, felt nothing like it for me. I was exhausted, freaked out, not sure of how to sit, stand, walk or even shit.

I knew that my hormones were working in overdrive and this was most certainly an understatement. I seemed to be struggling to hold back tears, but for what? The next days of waiting were stressful. Although I kept telling myself in some absurd way that "I am pregnant", in the back of my mind I knew full well that this was not the case. I really wanted the embryo to implant and grow! I wanted to be a mom! A couple of days went by and I began feeling stitching in the stomach, nausea, backache, dizziness. I had all of the symptoms. I actually had to make some awkward calls to find out how to stop this nausea because I had to get to work and it really would not be very polite if I upchucked all over my client. It really would not sit well at all.

D day had arrived! The bloods had to be taken. I was not sure of what to do, how to react with the news, what would the next step bring? we went through to Lancet at Vitalab where I gave my arm to the nursing vampire. Actually I found a good vein for her so that I would not feel any pain. The barcode was then handed to the loving and warm receptionist and we then opted to leave just in case we got bad news.

Time was marching on and my heart was beating quicker and quicker. I was nervous but I didn't want to call for results. As usual I felt that I did not want to be a burden and I was not sure how I would react on the phone so I left it. The frustration and anxiety was just building up and I could not take it any more. I knew the news could not be good. Just then the phone rang and then it hit me! " Negative", " it is a sad day, be sad but get up tomorrow!" I was given instructions to stop all medication and allow my body to naturally cleanse itself and to see the doctor on the arranged date. The phone went down and my life just caved in.

It felt like the rug was pulled out from under my feet and I had hit myself so hard. I was in absolute pain and I couldn't contain myself. I was ready, I wanted to be a mom! I wanted this now! He will leave me and I can't blame him because I am nothing. I mean nothing to anyone and I cannot open up. He is better off with someone else who will love him and give him kids. I cannot do it. I just kept crying and crying. All I actually wanted to do was hug my husband and cry in his arms. I do not remember when last I cried so uncontrollably and for so long. It is almost as if the fertility process has softened me and reduced me to a bundle of nerves and emotion.

On the Sunday after the incident, we went for coffee with my in-laws and in walked one of the counsellors from Vitalab. She said she would call the next day to organize a session for the two of us together. I was initially very apprehensive. This was something I had never done and wasn't one to talk about my feelings with those I didn't know. Why bombard others with this sort of shit? After some time and some soul searching, I felt that it would be irresponsible of me to bring a child into this world without sorting myself and my relationship out first. I needed to feel whole again. I needed to feel loved. Would I ever feel joy again after feeling like such shit for days after the implant didn't take? Was this a miscarriage? I wanted to move forward, I wanted to carry on with my life and hopefully try again but I needed to be alright first.

I understand now that I need to be more open with others but this means that I don't have to say certain things that are uncomfortable for me or say things just to please others. I also need to be more open in order to create deeper and better relationships. Time for loved ones, especially a spouse, is imperative. My bond with my husband is really strong and one that I cherish and would never want to break. It is a bond that not many people get to have in life. I want this bond to be even stronger and better than it is now. This means openness. Can I do it? I must do it!...

This was finally happening. We were going to get pregnant. Everything felt right. Everything was right. And then it wasn't.

I remember exactly where I was when Michelle called me to say that the IVF had not taken. Traffic was heavy as I was driving back from a client and my heart was breaking. Not just because I had thought that we would be having a baby in 9 months because in our minds, or at least mine, Mich must have been pregnant from the moment we saw a little flash of light on the scan - this was the embryo being inserted.

I can't explain exactly what it feels like when your wife, the love of your life, the person who you are meant to protect at all costs calls you sobbing uncontrollably and you cannot do anything to curb the pain. Heart attack. I felt like someone had a grip on my heart and was squeezing. The wind was sucked right out of my lungs. I couldn't see where I was going because my tears were blurring my vision.

The only thing that helped was getting home, climbing into bed with my wife and us holding each other while we cried. When we finished crying we were just sad, very sad. That lasted for what seemed like forever. We were able to move on because of each other. Michelle was protecting me just as much as I was protecting her.

Whoever said that time heals all wounds was a deluded idiot. Time heals nothing. It makes us numb and we learn to deal with the pain in a more manageable way. No, time doesn't heal at all – love does! No matter how tough you portray yourself as, never close yourself off to love.

Meeting My Angel

You never know what challenges others are going through – so just be nice!

IVF: Take 2

"It has taken me a good few months of hard work, soul searching and relationship building. I have finally decided that I am ready to jump back on the horse and make an appointment with Dr G to restart the process. I am now ready yet again to go through those early morning scans, drugs, appointments, poking and prodding. Hopefully this time will bring a different outcome. We both so deserve a different outcome and the hope is all we have to hold on to."

The day came for us to have our consult with Dr G and then a visit with the nursing coordinator. Naturally, I heard myself saying "Wait there's more! Drum roll please!" it appeared that my ovary produced an egg! Gasp! Oh my word! When I initially heard this I found it really hard to rap my head around this information. So much so that when the nurse told us what the scan showed, I said that I not did not understand what she was saying. As far as I was concerned, I had no eggs and I was not producing any either. "I am not getting you." I said. She very calmly sat and mentioned that of course she wanted to get the results of the blood tests first to make sure, however it seemed that there was a follicle. As usual, skeptical as ever, I still said it was a cyst and that I doubted it was anything more. Later that afternoon we got confirmation that it was most definitely a follicle. I tried processing this and it was undeniably difficult. I was absolutely ecstatic about all of this. However, the genetic component reared its ugly head yet again. We knew what the repercussions entailed if I fell pregnant with this follicle. We decided to make a choice and should there be good news, we would deal with the repercussions then.

December brought a lot of stress but also beauty and unity. Leave it to me to find a lump in my breast only days before my brother and sister in-law were to get married. One of my biggest fears! Where to now? I was a wreck! We managed to get an emergency appointment with the radiologist and of course my suspicions were confirmed. The cyst that turned out to be a follicle had now materialized in my breast. Somehow I managed to find a little water filled pocket that was so tiny even the radiologist was shocked that I managed to find it. We were extremely relieved! The rest of December was wonderful as I could really just spend time bonding with my other half, regrouping and relaxing at the pool. Exactly what was needed after a really tough year, or so I thought.

January came and work had started again. I was back in the swing of things. We had planned for the next IVF and now we were throwing a few new medicines into the mix that would hopefully help. We organized for Neupogen, which had to be injected straight into my cervix to be done. Apparently this aids in strengthening the uterus and egg implantation. We then also planned the transfer date and it was literally all systems go now. So daunting!

The 15th of January, a very significant day arrived. Why was this so significant? Well, wait and see. "I am meant to go through to Vitalab for Neupogen today and in a couple of days I am to have the transfer. I arrive for work at 7:30 as usual and begin with my usual routine. I know what work needs to be done before leaving and I set out on my usual busy schedule to get everything done. I have not been working too long since arriving in the morning and in walk six armed men. It took me a couple of moments before I realized that I was in the middle of a pretty serious hold up. After getting slapped and kicked, we are all locked in the bathroom, the key is thrown away and my laptop and phone are savagely taken from me. Once we are all rescued from the bathroom, I call Jared to let him know what has happened. He rushes over to fetch me and I refuse to let him drive me home. I know that I will have to go back to collect my car and I will not be in any position to do this anytime soon." Somehow in the back of my mind I knew something was going to happen to me, I just did not know when. It just so happened that the incident took place on a really important day in a really important week.

Jared managed to get hold of the in-house counselor from Vitalab for an immediate debriefing before I went for Neupogen to calm me a little. So I cried, I got home and bathed, cried my eyes out there too, had a quick sandwich, cried a lot more, got in the car and off we went immediately at 12 to be debriefed and of course then we walked straight over for Neupogen. Because of what I went through that morning the staff found it exceptionally difficult to deal with me. They tried everything to make me feel comfortable and relaxed. I knew that I had to do this. I had taken all of the medication and been scanned. All was on track. Except for my emotional and psychological state. That night I refused to speak to anyone. I only started making calls and speaking to people from the next morning and that was very difficult for me.

Over the next few days I do not know what I did or what happened. All I knew was when I needed to be at Vitalab for the transfer and had to try to relax. All I could do was breathe. We had to take a shot at this otherwise it was like pissing in the wind. Before the Neupogen and hold up I had been speaking to Jared about my concerns and how fearful I was about the transfer. The nerves were so bad that I felt physically ill. Thinking back, it was once again probably all the medication I was taking. Did I mention that I had to take estrogen tablets and patches, which are replaced every 48 hours.

Transfer day arrived and I made sure that my favorite relaxing music was pre-loaded onto my phone just to make sure I was chilled. Unfortunately no Def Leppard, Bon Jovi or Queen. It was all classical, which I have no problem with as I am a “muso” myself. I was determined to relax and just go with the flow as best I possibly could. That is a laugh though, because how are you supposed to relax when you have had such an incredibly messed up week as I had? I was imagining every possible way that the transfer was going to be messed up. I just had one question though. What happens if this transfer does not take? Unfortunately or fortunately, what kept going through my mind during the hold up was that I was expecting. Huh? I was meant to have the transfer this week but somehow I was being protected and watched closely by my guardian angel.

"I have been waking up at around 5 am. I have been dreaming about a gorgeous baby who is lovingly cuddling with me. His arms are wrapped around my neck and when the child is on the bed being changed, it is putting its hands close to my face, being kissed and cuddled, spoken to softly, loved, adored. Where on earth is this coming from? Am I hallucinating now? These meds are brilliant! A trip I will never forget!"

The day of the transfer and I was surprisingly calm. I actually think that the whole process has softened and relaxed me. Who would have thunk it, hey? The transfer itself was terrifying but at the same time awesome. Dr G controlled everything and we had a few extra visitors in the room to make sure that I held it together. What am I saying, pretty much the whole of Vitalab was present for the show.

The wait after the transfer was quite calm. I refused to be around negativity. We watched comedies, relaxed as much as we could and spoke in very even tones. However, I had started taking thirty minute sessions, a kind of guided imagery if you will. Basically I would close the door, turn the lights off, get nice and comfy on the bed and shut myself off from everything. I would shut my eyes and begin by focusing on my breathing. Breathe in, breathe out, breathe in, breathe out. I kept repeating this a few times. Then, I would start focusing on the noises around me. I would pick five different sounds to focus on. Then, I know I am quite deep into the imagery. I just needed to have the picture in mind. I had taken myself off to the most amazing, most beautiful places ever. In this particular situation all I kept on hearing was "mommy are you okay?" Words which for me, on their own, were tremendously powerful and longingly beautiful.

I then found out that my other half had a really disturbing dream that I miscarried. This obviously did not bode well. I took a thirty minute session later in the week and again I kept hearing this beautiful voice from a gorgeous little angel saying "Mommy, I am coming, can you see me? Mommy, look at me, I am coming." I was so confused and had no clue of what to expect. I just hoped that the embryo was growing as it should have been and that we would get the good news we deserved. All I could say to this gorgeous little angel was, "but where are you? I can't see you!" The child then pointed to my heart and said "I am in your heart." I was sobbing through the entire thirty minutes.

Finally D-Day! We arrived early for bloods to be taken. We decided to leave and go and get something to drink and come back for 8:30am. We were called in after a bit of a wait and I knew something was wrong. "Please sit guys. I have very bad news for you." All I could think was, "Shit not again!" I asked our coordinator "What do we do now?" and as advised I went to bed, took a script for the pill and organized to see a counselor. We had a few minutes to ourselves and I just broke. Jared was holding me and all I could think was that this really had not been a good start to the year at all. We got home and we both climbed into bed and held one another and cried. I guess the lesson here is that it is so important to listen to oneself and trust one's instincts, no matter how hard or how bad it may be. We are the masters of our own universe and somehow we all have that sixth sense, we just need to tap into it and just trust. You never know where you will end up...

Talk about a rollercoaster of trauma and emotions. That pretty much summed up the cycle leading up to the second IVF. Mich was a bundle of nerves. Her anxiety was so overwhelming that at times I didn't know what to do or how to calm her. It is hard for me to let go of wanting to always be there and it felt like this IVF cycle and all the horrific "add-ons" of Mich's lump and the attack were pretty devastating for me. I did what I could but having to ward off family, even her parents, whose intentions were positive left me reeling. All I knew was that my wife was coming apart at the seams and I was not getting any of the support I needed to comfort my wife and maintain my composure like I normally do.

I vividly remember the day of the attack how Mich needed to see a client of hers and I drove her and waited there so that she was not alone at any point. She was completely distressed, and I found myself getting angrier and angrier with the barrage of calls, advice, concern and intrusions that I was vetting on my phone. None of them seemed to realize that I was also traumatized. How could I not be when the person I love more than life itself was hurting so much and no-one really knew what I had been building myself up for over the next 15 days.

Positivity is crucial, perhaps for a positive result, but definitely for your own sanity as a couple going through fertility.

Ours had been severely compromised. We were not sleeping and eating properly and the dream I had left me feeling crushed. Somehow we managed to feel hopeful but at the same time felt like charlatans. It was as if we never expected a pregnancy from this attempt, but we were deluding ourselves into believing that it would happen. After all statistics say that IVF is successful on average every 1.8 attempts. Well we are certainly not average then.

Meeting My Angel

You never know what challenges others are going through – so just be nice!

IVF: Take 3

We are back to square one! For a moment during the hold up and my guided imagery sessions, I thought something is definitely there watching over me, protecting me. I have a guardian angel that I can talk to and see when I need to. How is it possible though that the voice, the message, the beautiful baby I was seeing is just not there? We were not expecting? Was it all a lie? I blame the medication, yeah that is it.

After all we have been through, the financial burden has been the larger of our problems that we have to deal with. Unfortunately that is what we deal with when going through fertility treatment. How do you put a price on a child, on children? For some it comes cheap and for others it is a long and expensive but immensely rewarding road.

I refuse to wait another four or five months before we have another transfer. However, I really just do not know what to do anymore and I really wish someone would just tell me. Anyone but my apparent guardian angel. There is this constant pressure to succeed, make money, do well in business, just push all the way.

However, we never give ourselves the opportunity to recharge and see the whole picture and at times it is difficult to see the whole picture while you are in such a tough situation. You just put your head down, hope the plane does not crash and you just keep going and doing what you need to do.

I am assuming we now begin the cycle again. The healing, the medication, the scans, the embryo thawing, no sex, patches, the IVF theatre. I am sure Dr G will probably throw something new in the mix but of course we will have to wait and see what happens at the next appointment. Sometimes I wish I could just flip a switch saying stop and it automatically changes the circumstances to positive, happy, or maybe just easier. This year has really started off in the most atrocious way possible. I have to now pick myself up, dust off and move on. For now, my dead eyes, my drained mind and vulnerable self need to deal with all that has happened and come to terms with everything. Let's see where we end up.

I asked Dr G if there was something wrong with me that we haven't picked up yet? It was an unequivocal no. Next time we try again, he has decided that it may be a good idea to put two embryos back. I am scared. I know if I end up with twins, I will be completely uncomfortable but I was assured that I would get the right medical care with the best doctors required if it comes to that. He gave me a big hug as we were leaving and he told me not to be too hard on myself and to give myself time and think about what I want and mostly give myself time to grieve and heal.

It took me some time and eventually I felt that I did not want to wait any more. I was ready. I really wanted kids and I wanted to get started again with the process. It felt almost like a new chapter in a book, where you could see the page being turned, with a new beginning waiting to bloom. Who knew what it would bring but I really want to find out.

My back unfortunately had been giving me quite a bit of trouble and I had been going for physiotherapy to try and ease the pain and tension. It was an old injury from my horse riding days and of course leave it to me to have that additional bit of trouble to deal with during this already very stressful time that we were going through. Did we need to go through anything more? Now really!!!

I know I have some sort of guardian angel or something watching over me and protecting me – at least I felt this way when I was in the armed robbery. I actually had a really awesome conversation with that child again during one of my guided imagery sessions. The conversation we had was amazing! He asked me if I would still love him and miss him when he grew up and left home. The other question was on what day of the week I want to have the baby and if he could be one of our babies. Of course, I was really happy with the questions and our conversation. He was so real! He looked almost exactly like my other half did when he was a toddler – he was a really cute, gorgeous little thing, however very different personality-wise. He seemed very close and very connected to me. I wonder if it is just because of the connection I have with these sorts of things or if this was truly someone I would experience a very strong and special bond with in the future – in reality. I felt so at ease with this child.

It seems like each time I have the transfer something gets in the way or throws everything out so that I am stressed, upset, traumatized or something else. I want to be able to enjoy this process. I know it is not meant to be easy. I know it is uncomfortable but I have chosen to see the positive in it. I am focused on the end goal. I feel calm knowing that the end result will be filled with love, beauty, children. This is what I want, what we want.

We organized an appointment and arrived on the Friday for the scan as arranged. Off I went to the bathroom as usual and I was directed to one of the scanning rooms. I proceeded to strip as usual, climbed up onto the bed and covered up. Doctor G began looking at the screen and instantly I knew something was wrong. The lining only reached 5.6 mm. This was not normal for me and certainly not at this stage of the game. I was told to get dressed and meet him in his office. When we got there Dr G was going through my file and closely looking at the previous reading. The lining was much thicker then. I was worried and very disappointed. How? Why? We were asked if I had been swimming in any lakes lately, or if I took any anti-inflammatories. The response was a resounding no!

Again I was pulled into one of the rooms and I did another quick strip tease. This time it was so we could do a biopsy. We needed to get to the root of this and find out what was going on with me. The biopsy was excruciating. I do not think I have ever been awake in a more physically painful situation than this. A local anesthetic was even administered and this unfortunately also did not help me. I just felt pain, scared and I was near to breaking Jared's hand. We had to move rooms as there were no stirrups in our examination room. So, I put the covers around me and I quickly did a hop into the next room. At this point I really did not blame Dr G who kept asking for a different cervix. I know I did not make things easy with my interesting anatomy. He did apologize a number of times because he knew he was hurting me. We tried different speculums to try and get a decent sample and it just did not work. Finally, after trying a few times and quite a bit of blood, Dr G managed to get a really good sample out of me. I saw the worm as it was called. Dr G bagged it, I got dressed and went to the lab to have bloods done. I had been put onto an antibiotic for a month and hopefully this would work.

When we finally got home I was completely disheartened, upset, hopeless and I began to cry. I had to start this process over again, that is if the process could continue. I was nervous that all our chances had ended! I really wanted the process to be successful. I needed it to be successful. We both wanted children! I was nearly there! I was so close to having the Neupogen, IV and transfer done and now this. So now we had to wait until we are able to see Doctor G. I did not know what to expect or think. I was tired, finished actually. I needed to find peace of mind.

The next time I was meant to get my period was not like usual. It was not an even flow and I was becoming more and more stressed at this fact. I was due to start taking the pill so we could begin the process and this made it so difficult for me to judge. Eventually, I could not take it anymore. Jared called in to Vitalab and organized for me to be scanned. I arrived, went to the bathroom and within a few minutes we were directed to the "special scanning room" where they usually deal with the more difficult stuff like biopsies, Neupogen etc. I climbed onto the bed and looked at my other half. We both were upset and in this darkened room, crying and trying to keep it together. Eventually we both dried our eyes and the doctor walked in. To our surprise the medication was working as hoped. My lining was thick! like a rope, clear, not like previously seen as tattered and scrappy. I was really happy! I was told when to begin the pill, finished my period off on day 6 and all worked out really well for once!

So, we had finally begun the process again. I was really excited to see what my body could do now that I had my blood pressure, glucose, cholesterol and weight under control. I had worked so hard and had come so far. I was given the usual jab in the backside, had a bleed and was told to begin taking the estrogen tablets and patches. I was scanned and all seemed fine, although the doctor wanted the lining thicker. As he has previously done, he told me to increase the dosage of estrogen as well as now having to take *shock horror* Viagra suppositories. It was so uncomfortable! I pulled myself together and began taking the medication and it was not so bad – just a bit stiff. I was bracing myself for the bad headaches, was ready with a box of Still-pain on my bedside pedestal and I thought I was going to be a right royal pain in the backside for the weekend. I really did not think I was as bad as all that. I was just really tired though but that was because of a lack of sleep. We were told to come back for another scan as doctor G wanted to see how things had progressed. The lining was worse. He seemed really perplexed and was not sure what had happened. Immediately I was told to go off the Viagra, continue with estrogen and the other medication and he wanted to see me on the Friday for a procedure. I knew there was something wrong. I even asked him when I got on the table to give me the bad news. I know my body and I know when something is not quite right.

The day for my procedure came. I was then taken in to theatre and Dr G was facing the screen busy looking at something very quickly. He warmly greeted me and we got the road on the show. The anesthetist took my left hand and started looking for veins that would cooperate. Dr G came to my other side, took my hand, held it and told me not to worry. He said "everything is fine and we are taking good care of you." I would not even know that they had been there at all. He calmed me some more with the usual chit chat we are used to. He was so good to me! I felt completely reassured and I have never had a doctor take my hand and stay with me till I was completely asleep. The anaethetist administering the gas asked me if the room was spinning yet, I replied and within 5 to 10 seconds I was gone, not even floating but completely gone!

I woke up after the procedure and doctor G explained everything to us. Apparently there was some kind of "restriction" and he managed to cut open a whole corner of my uterus that was flapped over the back. It seems like he made the area quite a lot bigger so hopefully the lining had space to grow nicely now. I had been put on medication to help with the recovery and he mentioned that he wanted a follow up with me.

We were all very hopeful that the coming transfer would bring a different result. The area was certainly bigger to carry a fetus. Here's to hoping!

So, the day had finally arrived for the transfer. I collected my medication and we went downstairs to get ready. I handed the Atociban drip to the nurse, filled out the paperwork, got dressed into the usual gorgeous robes and made myself comfortable on a lazy boy. When I had been on the drip for enough time and my bladder was pretty full, we were escorted through to theatre. My bladder was scanned and I was feeling uncomfortable as I needed to pee. Doctor G arrived and amused me to no end! He took a look at the screen and was really impressed with the lining! He even commented on how amazing it looked and he told the sister where and when to scan so he could find the right spot to put the embryos. Eventually we found the right space. Between all of us we eventually found out which side we had to use and I was shown the picture of the embryos. Wow! Apparently the one was pretty good looking and well developed, while the other was fragmented but now well developed and maybe just needed a space to grow and develop more inside me. We were not sure what would happen and we could only really hope for the best. I remember earlier that morning when I woke up, I asked G-d to be with us while the transfer was taking place. Once the transfer was done, I had to finish the last few minutes of the drip while my other half went to get my Clexane (blood thinner) injection so the nurse could show me how to administer it. I got dressed, was shown how to inject myself and then off we went to Dischem to collect the remainder of the injections, which would be taken for the next twelve days and hopefully longer.

I was told to expect spotting. I was also a little moody and tearful at times but not like before. I was really not sure of what to expect. I was hoping all was fine and would go according to plan but unfortunately that is something, I have come to learn, that is not in my power. I was still getting mixed thoughts about the results. I really wished that this wasn't the case!

I acknowledged that it was difficult for me to find a connection with the embryos and although I wanted to have the time to be alone for a bit to be able to connect,

I never managed.

Unfortunately or fortunately, before you know it, the day for bloods to be taken is knocking on your front door. We tried our usual approach, go for bloods early, get coffee – or in my case rooibos tea – and rush back to get results. Finally we were called in and told to sit down. The door was closed and I looked up at Anne and she just shook her head. "Sorry Mich.... it is not positive." I was completely stumped! Speechless! It was difficult to process and understand what had just happened. I took a moment and still nothing. She showed me the paper and nothing. I processed and thought to myself there was nothing more or less that I could have done to make this work. We all did what we could have and everything went as planned.

At the end of the day it was just not the right time. It was not meant to be then. But it will. It will be, when it is meant to and it is coming soon. I know it is. The souls have been chosen and I will never stop looking for them until I find them. This will work ...

How do you as the husband, the "rock" in the relationship, cope knowing that you and your wife want nothing more than to be parents; to hold an innocent little life in your arms – and no matter how hopeful and determined you are it is just not happening. You have promised your unborn child, the love of your life and yourself that you will do everything in your power to protect and look after your family, but it remains just the two of you.

It is ridiculously difficult! Especially for men, or at least ones like me. I have always been a "softie" and really love children, perhaps because I am a big child at heart. They are precocious, inquisitive, imaginative little people who teach us so much about how beautiful and precious life is once we get past the mumbo jumbo that we tell ourselves is important. Up until this point there have been several challenges that I have been wrestling with.

Challenge number one for me has been dealing with the fact that we are not hearing that infectious giggling that we thought we would within the first few years of our married life – unless you count our own. Laughter and finding ways to make each other smile has helped us get through so much already. We are so ready to be awesome parents. We have overcome so much already and we are so determined but this was like a social tennis player coming up against an on song Roger Federer or Raphael Nadal. No matter what we try we are being drilled. Neither Michelle nor I like losing, especially me. Trying naturally, unnaturally and supernaturally (and by that I mean praying) and still seeing no results has a profound effect on one's morale, wellbeing and beliefs. But despite my naturally emotional temperament I had to be strong or Mich would have crumbled by now. She has been hanging on going through a seemingly endless, repetitive cycle of hope and despair. And so my second great challenge has been created. How do I protect my wife from the pain and anguish that she has so obviously been feeling.

Anyone who knows me, knows how I hate seeing others suffer. Ever since I was little, this has been a core element in my being. I have always wanted to help and protect others not always realizing that overdoing it can come across as condescending and patronizing. Now imagine how much more protective I have become to ensure that my person does not get hurt any more than she already has been in this life. The trouble is that I am powerless, impotent, completely useless in doing the one thing that I had promised Michelle I would do. How can I? I can't will a child into existence. It has gotten to the point where I am hoping beyond hope that the visions that Michelle is having are going to come true; that Dr G is going to sink that impossible 80 foot putt that will allow us to have the family we have given everything for; for me to have my wife, my partner, my love back!

Who can I tell this to? No-one! I am a talker. I have even been told that I talk too much, which is probably me making up for the fact that I was so painfully quiet when I was young. Now I cannot tell anyone how I am feeling and why - because I am honoring and protecting Mich in the only way I really can. You see, she does not want to share our fertility challenge with anyone. She is so fearful of what stupid things people might say, ranging from pity to idiotic comments and even more reckless advice. And I cannot blame her but I need to express myself verbally to release some of my own pain. I can't always speak with Mich about this. I am supposed to be supporting her, not the other way around! This could have been the plot for Catch-22.

Despite all of this, 3 IVFs down the road and we are still standing – somehow. Are we giving up? Not a chance! Is it because we are suckers for punishment;

twisted masochists? Definitely not! I have always believed that we are given what we can handle. For some people that is a few drops, for others it is huge waves and then for others it is a series of relentless tidal waves. Someone believes that Mich and I can handle a whole lot more than we ever thought we would sign up for.

Meeting My Angel

You never know what challenges others are going through – so just be nice!

IVF: Take 4

Butterflies according to Japanese symbolism is indicative of the departed souls of loved ones. Interesting, and I think very true as well. I decided to look this up as I had been seeing fortunes of butterflies wherever I was. I absolutely love butterflies but this to me had a much deeper meaning. Of course, leave it to me to think about how much more rewarding it would be if only those souls knew how much they were loved and wanted.

So for the umpteenth time, I am looking forward to starting the process again. I went in for a Beriglobin and Gonapeptyl injection on Wednesday – the drugs sound like they are right out of a children's fairytale. Everything is timed, dated and of course set as an alarm on my phone. I just seem so angry though. Life has not been fare to us at all. The finances have been building up and there are more payments that need to be made. It is just one thing after another.

I am pretty nervous about starting everything again, as I want everything to be perfect and I know that perfect is not always achievable, especially with my genetic background and unique uterus. During our morning scan Dr G commented that he was really happy with my uterus. It was really wonderful to know that I did not go through all the pain for nothing. Yes, I inherently know this but sometimes it seems that I need to hear it and actually say it to myself in order to truly believe it. Yes, I know, I need to trust my intuition and feelings. My intuition has helped me on so many occasions, I just need to listen to myself more. It's just that sometimes I need a more professional opinion. It is not confirmation for me it is more like getting the facts from the horse's mouth.

I took a thirty minute session. It started with me focusing on my own inhalation and exhalation, which was followed by a picture of the earth. The "camera" then moved closer into earth, then the continent and eventually I was seen sitting on a rock. There were tears streaming down my face and I was sitting on the beach in Scottburgh on a boulder. This beautiful image made me remember that there is a bigger plan out there for us all. We cannot control what will be! It is a plan set and made for each one of us by the big man. I firmly believe this. As much as I try and fight it and get impatient, I still most definitely believe this.

I know that our time is coming. We will have kids. This is a path that has definitely been set for us. Following the teary session, I then saw myself walking on this sunny, godly, golden path and I was joined by my husband and two little ones holding my hand and Jared's hand. It was really a beautiful picture watching the four of us walking together into the sunlight on this golden path. I know we have to continue along this path and we will eventually get to where we need to be. I also know that the end goal is most important and I must keep it in mind. Having children is what I am concentrating on at the moment. However, and grudgingly accepting of this, I know that it will happen when it is meant to.

I had another opportunity to take a thirty minute session. I saw Jared and me walking into the IVF theatre. He was holding my hand and in my other hand I was pulling my Atociban drip. I was in scrubs ready to have the procedure done. I climbed onto the bed and was scanned by the nursing sister. As usual everything was as it should be. Yes, everything was intact and there were no additional appendages that I needed to worry about. I then saw Dr G mixing and measuring the sedation for the drip and administering it. A sense of calm came over me. So much so that I was almost numb. I do not know what to expect from this procedure and I am scared. Without my mental and physical interference, Dr G could now calmly and happily insert the embryos. Initially I thought I saw the embryos frowning. In the next part of the "clip" I saw Jared and myself sitting in Anne's office and she was telling me that again the embryos did not take. A bit too prophetic for my liking hey? Of course I was upset, crying. I recall myself staring at the page with the information from my bloods. This was exactly the way I had reacted before. I was angry and upset and as usual, I asked "what now?", to which Anne responded "have a bleed, go to bed, today is a sad day so be sad and get up tomorrow." I asked the exact same question as I did previously. "Is there anything we are missing?" The answer is a resounding no!

Of course this was in my thirty minute session and I did not want to create a self-fulfilling prophecy. So, in reality, once again we arrived on the day of transfer. I was undoubtedly nervous, but I still managed to keep it light-hearted and relaxed. My drip was going well and, after a while, I was called through to theatre to check how full my bladder was. The nursing sister,

Evie, said it was pretty full and called the doctor immediately. Jared had to quickly put stuff away in a locker so I bravely walked into theatre alone where I would wait for him on 'shpielkes'. I just wanted him to be with me while the procedure was happening and naturally I worried that somehow, stupidly in the back of my mind, he would not be in. He was though, but only once I was covered up and my bladder was checked. Once the doctor arrived everything went so quickly! He gave me a bit of Dormicum in my IV drip followed by the "milk of amnesia", apparently a soya milk concoction. There I am lying on the bed thinking this shit doesn't work and it won't knock me out, I can take it and I can fight it, I am strong. The moment he started inducing me, the concoction began working and, oh boy, was it amazing! Immediately, my head and the room began to spin and then I was completely out. Apparently there were jokes about me having a super liver because they had to top me up with the sedation quite a few times. I apparently metabolized the stuff really quickly it seemed. The next thing I remember, I was being wheeled into the recovery room and I remember asking the doctor how it went and he responded that it went well. Someone also told me that I must talk to the embryos. I don't know who it was. I was completely out of it. Following the procedure, we waited a few minutes for the IV to drain, I got dressed, went to the bathroom and we went upstairs to see our nursing coordinator. All I remember is that this time felt very different to the previous transfers. I don't know what will happen with the results of this transfer. I just cannot wait to meet these two beautiful, naughty, gorgeous little angels in 8 months time. I am really blessed. I don't feel much actually. Apparently everyone cheered when the doctor got the embryos in place. It was as if it was the perfect place for them and everything was calm. I would have liked to be awake but honestly I am much happier that I wasn't because maybe somehow I was blocking the transfers before. Maybe he had to sedate me to be able to put the embryos where he wanted to without worrying about me and my thoughts. Dr G is human too and I am so thankful that he did the transfer.

Since the transfer, I haven't really felt anything. Previously, I would feel almost bloated or something just didn't feel right. Now it feels like it is part of my body and I am comfortable. I am not in pain. Sometimes I feel a stitch or something funny, maybe pulling but on the whole not bad at all. I was really dizzy for a couple of days and this was probably from my hormones. I just hope all goes well and we can start the next phase of our life now. I imagined us getting ready to welcome a beautiful human or humans into this world. I was trying to imagine how they would like their room to look. I even recall asking them if they like the music I play on Classic FM. There was a weird situation where I introduced them to the person that just left the room after having a chat with me or someone else around me. I even disciplined them this morning telling them to be nice to their doggies. Have I gone batshit crazy or what?

I took a look at the list of meds and the date for bloods. I noticed that again there was no follow up date for an appointment with Doctor G. This actually freaked me out a little because my mind starts working overtime and it runs away with itself. I told Jared and he as usual looked at the positive side of it and then we shared a really nice warm hug. Honestly, I think I am worried because it feels like nothing is there. What happens if I forget that I am "pregnant" and do something I am not meant to? Then I remember that I had the transfer and I can count on that to tense up yet again. In general I am trying to keep as calm as possible and not feed into any negativity or nonsense.

The arrival of D-Day came with a bang. No, not literally. As our usual patterns would have it, we woke up early and made sure we arrived for bloods to be taken for 7am. The stringent, controlling, time-bound girl, hopefully soon to be a mom found this to be more relaxing and easier to cope with. When I removed my top, sat down and looked at the needle, all I could think was "now they are taking my blood". It was almost as if my mind was elsewhere, blank almost and then this kind of jolted my mind straight back to reality. There is nothing like a blood test to smack you on the back of the head and say "WAKE UP!" The barcode was given to one of the ladies at the front desk and off we went for tea and a dose of Clexane and some other 'cocktail' drugs. We returned to Vitalab for 9:15. We sat for a couple of minutes and I remember one of the girls escorting us through to one of the nursing sister's room's. All I remembered were the words "come my love, Veli will see you now." No one ever calls me this and for once it felt comforting, warm. This to me was possibly a comfort that made me realize there and then that something was wrong. We got to Veli and everything was a blur. I just remember her saying

"Guys, I don't have good news for you."....

I immediately shut down. The walls began to close in on me. The sound of something shattering, my heart maybe, loudly resounded in my being. "What? But why? What on earth is going on?" The only thing I could say was "this is bullshit!" I was furious! I just could not understand what happened. We were all stumped like before.

Unfortunately, I think this is now more serious than we ever thought. This controlled, shattered life sat in the chair turning off all of the alarms that were now, once again, not required. Seeing that there was also no follow up appointment made on the printed sheet, Veli said that she would need to chat to Dr G to see where he could fit us in. Fuck! Now what?...

Basically we know the sperm can fertilize the eggs and the eggs are growing to day five or six. We are not sure however, if my uterus is able to carry and accept the eggs and if they are, are we possibly missing the right time for the fertilized eggs to be put back there? So many questions! They now have to grow my endometrium for the umpteenth time. I will be on the usual course of medication and once I have reached the stage where they are ready to usually do the IVF procedure, the doctor is going to do a scrape of my lining and send it to the lab to see if we are in the correct window period and hopefully we can see what we are doing wrong. If results come back saying that we are in the correct window period and the eggs are just being let through, then the answer is that my uterus is simply just not accepting the embryos. Essentially, if this is the outcome then it means we either have to do the GIFT, ZIFT or adoption. Doctor G is getting worried now, which is unsettling for me because he doesn't usually get phased. He said he doesn't want to gamble and just put the embryos back. He wants to be perfectly sure that he is doing everything he possibly can for us. The outcome is not exactly what we planned. What am I saying?! It is nothing like we planned. However, it seems that there is still a glimmer of hope. Dr G even said he has a feeling that maybe we are just putting the eggs back a day or so early or too late and we are just missing the window. We must remember that Dr G is putting the eggs back as if I were a normal case. From the start we all knew that I was not going to be an easy case but this is now becoming ridiculous! ...

This was our fourth attempt at adding to our family. Mich's guided imagery sessions had given her a greater sense of calm and often we would discuss these, what she saw, felt, heard, smelled and tasted. The visions she had were so real and although I was not experiencing these myself other than Mich recounting them, they felt so real to me too. The children she was describing, their sweet precocious natures were ours – we just had to meet in person in this world.

I loved talking about what she saw in her "30 minutes sessions"; having Mich ask me what I thought and regaining the real hope that I would genuinely be walking towards her with two tiny hands in my own. Her visions were more than that. They were real and these beautiful souls that she had met were just waiting to be united with us. Most importantly for me, I felt more like my old self leading up to the days of the IVF. We were enjoying each other's company in a way that we hadn't done properly in a while. We were starting to become the really awesome people we know we are but had been too caught up in the never-ending saga of one IVF after another interspersed with drugs, scans, consultations and payments to let them emerge.

Not for one moment have I regretted a single decision that I have made of anything we have tried to this point. What I did regret was not always being completely emotionally available for Mich because of the private battle I had been going through and trying to hide from the world. Only two people other than Mich knew just how rough this had been for me as well, my parents. My dad would let me come to him to talk and would not try to confront me on how I had been feeling, while my mom always used to check in with me in her own gentle way.

Having a relationship with someone other than your partner, where you can "unload" and speak openly, is essential. That might be a friend, a family member, a cleric or even your hairdresser or barber. The point is that if you bottle absolutely everything up you ultimately become useful to no-one. Find that outlet. Create some space for yourself. Both to mourn and to heal.

Meeting My Angel

You never know what challenges others are going through – so just be nice!

Oops We Did It Again... We Just Had To!

It is a week after the news. We have spoken to the doctor and he has given some hope, but I am still not feeling it. Honestly, I am feeling pretty despondent, and I am not confident that this last stage of the process will work. It is a long shot and I am very worried. I think both Jared and I are freaking out but not outwardly showing it or at least Jared is not. The park has been somewhat of a saving grace for us lately. I know all of this is not in my control. It never has been and it never will be. Sometimes it is actually a blessing that we can not control everything but sometimes, like in this situation; we want to be able to control it. Unfortunately, I am at a loss now and I just have no clue of what to do any more.

As each day passes, I feel a little stronger. I took a thirty minute session and again, I saw those two beautiful little children. I know that this is in the spiritual realm. I know this is not reality, but I so badly want them to be in the physical realm and I just do not know how to do this. While spending time with these two amazing angels, playing, laughing, enjoying, holding them, one of the kids started having a go at me. The kids asked me directly in a very serious tone, why I do not believe in them. "I am alive and here. You don't believe in us!" I was stumped. For once, this was a really difficult question to answer truthfully. It was hurtful and yet so hopeful and sincere at the same time. All I could answer was that I do believe in you. Although it is very difficult to believe when they are not physically present in the here and now. I am doing everything in my power to get them here and I just do not know anymore. I think even the doctor doesn't know any more. This last run is basically to just see if my uterus is viable and can accept a pregnancy.

I am out of sorts at the moment. Nothing is going as planned. I am pretty anxious about the way forward; upset because I am still not expecting; happy because I still have a loving and supportive husband; angry with the world and myself; frustrated because nothing has happened; and things are taking so long. Unfortunately, the fertility waiting game is one which we have had a fair amount of practice in. I really wish something would just happen.

I was sitting and decided that if the children are not meant to be for us then I should give them to someone who will love and cherish them as they should be. This is where it gets really weird now! The next thing I noticed that they were in the bath with me enjoying playing with boats, splashing around and of course tons of laughter and shrieking. This is all I have wanted for so long! I made a personal decision to visit the Mikvah with this specifically in mind and also to try and find someone who is able to do reflexology or some sort of alternative therapy on me to possibly "release" something.

Anyway, I have been quite frustrated and I just can't place certain emotions and things at the moment. We currently have two embryos left in the freezer. I am very sure we will have to choose a new donor considering our history and track record at Vitalab. Hopefully following the biopsy, we will have a better understanding of what my body is doing or not doing. Every time things get a little tough, I want to give up and run and convince myself that I am not cut out for this. Maybe I am not meant to be a mom, maybe this is not my path?

Considering how frustrated I am, what makes things even worse is that each time I take a thirty minute session, I either ask to see my kids or they just appear out of nowhere. They are gorgeous and we have the most amazing time together. Yes, I know this sounds completely nuts. I cannot help it, I am seeing them, touching them, feeling them, just the same as I am able to with those around me physically. It is just soul-wrenching to see these two beautiful children playing with me, arguing with me and one another and I just cannot experience it in reality. On the other hand this keeps me hopeful; it keeps me motivated and I wont stop until I manage to meet them in reality. I will do everything in my power to find those children and have them meet their dad. I just wish he could also see how beautiful they are. They look so healthy, happy and do not stop talking and are lovely, cheerful children. The time I have managed to spend with them has been nothing short of amazing. We bond for ages. We dress dolls, play hide and seek, lie on blankets and talk near waterfalls, chase after each other at the beach. Then of course I have also seen them playing with a really gorgeous golden Labrador puppy.

Once the thirty minutes is over and I am back to reality, I miss being with them, although they say they are in my heart. It just hurts me that they are not here and this fuels my fire to keep hoping and searching for ways to bring them into our reality. Of course I know this is not the 'run of the mill' case. No one ever accused me of being 'run of the mill'. I never have been. I am quite spiritually inclined and I have always been able to hear, feel and see things that other people may not be able to. For as long as I can remember, this has been my gift, and in some cases a curse. I try to fit in and be a normal, kind person. However, people actually do not know just how different I truly am. Not only have I got this Mosaic Turner's Syndrome, which makes me look a bit funny, I am also able to hear, see and feel things that others can not. Mutant? Yes I think so!

I sit here working at my desk, typing these words, listening to the constant whirring of the urn, the faint screeching from the fridge and the birds chirping outside. There is so much more to life than meets the eye. We are all on a path and controlled like puppets by G-d. He plans everything! With a mere 'swish of his finger' he controls all. Although we think we are in control of our lives and we go about our mundane business on a daily basis and exist, trying to create a legacy for future generations, He orchestrates and plans everything. He is in control and he decides what happens to you, whether it's good fortune, love, health or wealth, and of course the negative sides as well. It is just not in our control.

Having said this, it is so difficult to just let things go and to let it be and relax. I am very proactive and just want to fix things and make everything right. I do not know if I will be able to do this here but I will damn well try. After discussing with Dr G, the acupuncture sessions are simply to take the edge off. Of course we will add in a bit of psychological relaxation as well because lets face it, I am just a tad difficult at the moment. I am willing to be open-minded and of course enjoy the relaxation and time spent on me for me. I mean its great having sex and being around my husband and loving one another but I think sometimes we have to do things for ourselves in order to get better and be a better person. It really is a value-added benefit that you are providing for your spouse. But honestly, I am truly hoping that acupuncture can release the energy and get my blood and energy moving in an optimal way that will be positive for the babies. I am sure it will also relieve some mental stress, frustration, sadness etc. that has been chipping away at me as well lately. Sometimes unfortunately, you just do not know where to turn or what to do. The only thing you can manage is to just put your head down, breathe and hope everything will be alright in the end once you rise after the storm.

We have now arrived at the day before Neupogen and five days before the biopsy. I am actually feeling alright. Usually, I would be more anxious, flying off the handle, in attack mode or something else. I actually seem unusually chilled, which I am happy about don't get me wrong, but it is weird!

D-Day for the cervical strengthener arrived. I was lying there on the bed, covered up, waiting for Dr G to attend to me. As instructed, drank quite a bit – unfortunately no alcohol though – and was wanting to empty my bladder. Remember that Neupogen has to be administered on a fullish bladder and injected straight into the cervix in order to work properly. It does not end there. You have to wait a further 20 to 30 minutes after the injection so that the medication can spread and penetrate the area that it needs to. Finally, Dr G arrived and got the speculum he needed and tried to insert it into my uterus. Unfortunately, because of the nature of my condition, my uterus is not a normal one. It is 'squiff' and we deal with it. I was given a local, was watched very carefully to make sure I was alright and once he was done, he wished us well and said we must just hold thumbs for Monday. I feel there is no need. Hashem is now intervening and everything will be alright, better than alright. I said to him, “no all will be fine and this is happening”. I believe it completely and all will work out well for us. He was happy and confirmed the next transfer was again to be a sedated one. He must do what he needs to in order to make this happen. Of course I would like to see exactly what is going on, but otherwise I am happy with the way it is going. We need to do the biopsy. From there we will know how many days we are out of the window period and we will be able to hopefully have greater results from there.

So the day came for the biopsy and following the procedure I wasn’t in as much pain as I thought I would be. We were told to send a message two days later to see if results had arrived yet and still no response. Thursday came and admittedly the anxiety was most definitely there. I know somehow, I have been assured that we will have children. I am very open and willing to accept these two gorgeous angels and I know they are definitely coming.

The results had finally arrived and there were a few different options that were mentioned that we could follow in order to have children. Option 1, and the nicer option was that we are putting the embryos back at the wrong time. The second option was that we may have to go for the GIFT if my uterus doesn't accept pregnancies. Then there is ZIFT, adoption and surrogacy. Personally I know that I would want nothing more than to carry and give birth to my own children. I do not want complicated. Financially, it will be a strain if we have to go with the GIFT or ZIFT or the likes thereof.

So finally the day arrived. Apparently we have been about two or so days out of the cycle. This was amazing news because it means that there isn't something more serious like my uterus not being able to take embryos or pregnancies, which would have been really difficult to deal with. We were all really very happy! Of course if we go GIFT, this will remove all the issues and boom pregnancy. However, it is so expensive and I prefer to take the easier approach for now. I feel we should try again with the sedation and IVF, see what happens and we move from there. For now, I am just savoring the moment, enjoying the fact that I actually can carry my own babies, or so I think, and that I am going to carry them very soon. I am really looking forward to it and I know, so is my other half.

I am on break from acupuncture until we begin the process again. I was away for a day short of three weeks. In the coming week, I am already beginning with the injection phase. Next is to take my last Biphasil pill, have a bleed and immediately on day two I begin estrogen, scans and we are cooking. From when we saw Dr G, the process in all with the cycle of Biphasil was going to take 7 weeks, which is not very long when you think of all that we have to do. The body preparation is what takes time. Apparently, not everyone has the same length in cycles. They were initially thinking my body is the same as other females, which is over a twenty eight day cycle. No! Mine is confirmed now to be a little longer. We are just happy that there is no need for more serious action at this stage.

Apparently I have a very high tolerance for the 'milk of amnesia'. I woke up during conscious sedation while the doctor was doing the egg transfer and I had to be topped up with the medication. The next 12 days following were a mix of being relaxed to being very anxious that the result again would be negative. Well, lo and behold, we were both very nervous yesterday and when we were called in after the blood test, I looked straight at Anne and she shook her head. I had nothing left to say. I do not think it was me in shock. It was more the fact that I felt like I was going completely nuts. As I sit here writing, with tears in my eyes and wondering exactly why this cruel trick was played on us, I am strapped for words and do not know the way forward now. Jared has told me that under no circumstance can we afford to have the GIFT if we are financing it as well. I haven't included the fee for a new batch of donor embryos, unfrozen and frozen.

I just don't know what to do anymore. I wanted this to happen! It was in the bag! It was confirmed! I saw the lotus. I spoke with the Angel Gabriel. It was a really cruel trick played on us especially now between Rosh Hashana (The Jewish New Year) and Yom Kippur (The Jewish Day Of Atonement). How can I believe in angels anymore? I was showed a beautiful picture of two gorgeous children and now? Nothing! Of course if we want kids we will have to go with GIFT I think but the cost is not possible for us to afford at all...

If you have gone through any major life challenge and gotten back up time and time again you will know how draining it can be – psychologically, emotionally and physically. Fertility treatment takes this to another level, though. Once you have gotten up for countless early morning scanning appointments with your partner; cleared out your bank account for treatments, procedures and meds; prayed; cried and thought up any number of ways to throw others off the scent that you are trying to have a baby by any means necessary, there is still the fact that statistics are not in your favor and despite your best intentions you are just not in control. Lack of certainty nearly broke us. The worst thing that you can ever feel is not anger or shame. Your worst enemy is something far more powerful and insidious. Its name is hopelessness.

You can end up feeling hopeless at any point. Some people arrive at a fertility clinic feeling this way and some feel it after their fifth attempt. Do whatever you can to shatter this mindset as soon as possible because you are no use to yourself or others if you are depressed, sapped of all your energy and vitality. That little person needs a happy, healthy and loving family and they are totally dependent on you. You always have a choice. But as we sat in Dr G's office with our last shot with this batch of eggs, that is exactly how we felt. The only things that I tried that seemed to help me feel a little more positive was finding out more about our options and being kinder to myself.

I thrive on learning all the time - often "useless" information that I find some way to apply in my life but now I was doing this so I could be the dad I always thought I would be. That meant surfing the internet, reading articles and studies on IVF, GIFT, ZIFT, surrogacy and adoption. I knew I could not possibly know nearly as much as the doctors and staff at Vitalab. I just wanted to know enough to try and regain some semblance of control and to ask questions that the real doctors and experts could possibly help us to answer. I think what I really wanted was for us to know why this was not working for us and what we could do. What we got was care and support and let me tell you that was far more valuable than finding out the why.

It also made me realize how tough we had been on ourselves. We always tried to show the world how positive we are but that "bravery" wears you down. I needed to just be kinder to myself and Mich did too.

Fertility is the most grueling test of everything you have and your commitment to each other but you simply cannot do that if you are burnt out.

And boy did we need it. This was the fifth time that we had been in the theatre, the fifth time that Mich and I had had to prepare ourselves for what could be and the fifth time that we heard those dreaded words. Where to now???!!!

Meeting My Angel

You never know what challenges others are going through – so just be nice!

A New Start? Methinks Not!

We have been given profiles to look through so we could choose a new donor for the next step. I seem to feel more confident with the choice. The eggs are apparently reserved, frozen and waiting for our payment and of course implantation. We are able to go through with the new cycle and process immediately because a portion of the finances have been made available to us. However I am reserving judgement to see what the fertility fund requires of us. When you have reached a level of this sort of desire and desperation, you are prepared to do anything! It just so happens that Malka Ella is an organization that is so willing to help and are so very generous and so kind! I certainly consider ourselves very lucky!

We began filling the form out for Malka Ella. I was feeling a bit deflated actually. As usual, I was really worried that this would not work. We had only one choice moving forward – we had to do GIFT or ZIFT. My mind kept turning on the fact that this procedure is done laparoscopically. Of course I would have a proper anesthetic and not feel the pain, however I was bracing myself for the after effects. I was unsure if it was worth going through all this pain if the outcome might not change. I did not know what to believe any more. I had confirmation that this had a really good chance of working. If the procedure worked, well then of course it would all be worth it but unfortunately none of us know what the end result will be with anything in life, much less fertility treatment.

So I made the necessary preparations to meet with Anne to plan when I could begin taking medication, scans, and other appointments at Vitalab. She then called me to tell me that Doctor G wants to change the protocol with me if I was happy to do so. He wanted to see if it was possible to thicken my lining sufficiently in the hope that I produce a follicle naturally and without medication. Honestly, I thought we were wasting time here. He wanted to give me the opportunity to go through a mock cycle in the hope that it would work and then I would go straight into the procedure. It just felt to me that this opened us up for more disappointment and I had literally had enough of that. I was willing to try though. If he wanted to give me every opportunity to make sure everything had been given a bash, who was I to argue?

The day has very quickly arrived for the procedure to take place. It is year end and I am finishing off with my last few clients of the year, acupuncture, gym, tummy bug and theatre. Going through a full anesthetic, I was not allowed to eat or drink from 12pm the night before. We are up at 5am to get washed, dressed, let the dogs out to do their business, pack my bag, take the necessary medication and off we go to Vitalab to arrive for 7am. We march straight through to see Anne at 7:30, where we confirm how many embryos have been successfully fertilized. We then rush downstairs quickly to get ready for the procedure because they are taking me in at 8am. Together with baited breath, we walk into the IVF ward where I am directed to my little alcove. This was to be my recuperation corner after the procedure. Forms have to be filled out for the anesthetist so that I come out in tip top shape. I quickly put the scrubs on, take the medication I had been instructed to and off I go into theatre. Katherine was there with me. She is one of the nursing coordinators from upstairs. This lady is really amazing! So calm! I nearly didn't recognize her with her scrubs on. It is really comforting to see a familiar face downstairs with me. I then climb onto the bed again and have a chat with Pete my anesthetist. He has quite the sense of humor. The ladies are busily buzzing around me trying to organize the covers to secure my left arm during the operation so that when I am turned on my head, my limbs would not be flying around. Yip!!! Michelle is going to do a levitated headstand! Once properly secured and restrained *Roar*, Katherine then takes my hand and asks if I was ready. All the while my right arm is being prepped by Pete. He is organizing an IV for me, which I think is packed with a mild sedative. My blood pressure is now pretty low as the medication had already started flowing through my uncooperative veins. Then like a whirlwind, in walks Dr G. He says good morning to us all, makes a funny and then turns to me and says that we currently have 5 fertilized eggs, how many would I like to put back? I think for a moment and then respond with two. He then asks Jared and he also says the same. The consensus is the same all round, with doctors and patients. Now for the '*piece de resistance*'! Pete puts the oxygen to my face then begins injecting the anesthetic into the IV. Katherine turns to me and says goodnight or sleep well.

I woke up a while later in the bed, in pain. Jared was very gently rubbing my right hand and Pete was talking to him. All of a sudden I was unable to breathe. I thought I was going to die. I had something that felt like water in my mouth blocking my ability to breathe. I pointed there immediately and Pete knew he had to remove whatever it was immediately. I had apparently aspirated and I did not like that one bit! Finally I could breathe easily without this feeling of suffocation and impending doom. I remember flicking Jared's hand away like it was an annoying fly. I was thinking that Pete was a shitty doctor. Did he do something during the procedure that I did not like or was it the pipe in my mouth that freaked me out? I think this was the reason. I was just sore! Immediately I felt overcome with this wave of emotion and I just wanted to cry but somehow I could not. Jared kissed me and asked me if I wanted some water. My mouth was really dry and slowly I managed to polish off the glass. I really just wanted to go home! I was not allowed to leave until I went to the toilet and until Doctor G saw me and made sure I was alright. My blood pressure was checked and I was told to come get it checked a week later because it was quite high. Of course this was because I was being pumped with saline. I got up, did what I needed to, got dressed, saw the doctor, Anne for my injections and off we went home to sleep and recover. I knew the next two weeks were not going to be easy but at least now I was on holiday and I did not have to worry about the usual things.

The two weeks went by. We watched some great shows at home, went for dinners, went to different places looking for pool chairs and spent time basking in one another's company. We went to check my blood pressure a week later. Again it was high and the nurses could not understand why. Doctor G then told them to change the cuff and voila! my blood pressure was perfect. I know my blood pressure. I know I worry and I know that they scare me when they mention blood pressure. During all of this, I also had to have my stitches removed. I was in agony, but I knew the stitches were tight because Doctor G did not want the scarring to be bad. He had been nothing short of phenomenal!

The day finally arrived for the test like a clap of thunder. We were up at the usual time, 7am, had breakfast, meds at the correct time and off we went to the Linksfield clinic to brace myself for a fight with another vampire. I didn't seem overly nervous. When my blood had been taken, we walked out to the car and my eyes began to swell with tears. I couldn't hold them back. I knew what was to be expected and that it was not a baby. Jared tried to comfort me, he dried my eyes, told me I was so brave and we went on to do some errands. I paged the nursing staff and I left the message as we had been told to. We then waited patiently for the call. We decided to go and get some coffee and while I was sitting and sipping on my rooibos tea, the call came through that the results were again negative. As usual, I was to stop medication, have a bleed and begin the pill on day three of my period. What a loss! We left and went for a drive through to Illovo. The silence in the car was deafening. We didn't know what to say to one another. I tried to make sense of all of this and for a split second I heard these words ***"it is not about deserving, it is about appreciating what we have here and now and working with it."*** Yes, appreciation and acceptance of what one has is important. I do not think this is going to happen for us!

I do not think we have a chance of having children unless there is a surrogate or we adopt. Unfortunately, this is the case. I have given up and there is nothing I or we can do any more. The doctors' don't even know what to do any more. I truly hoped that this procedure would be different. I was even having different visions but it's all bullshit anyway. I am seeing things that are simply not there, simply not happening, simply and clearly are not meant to happen! It's hurtful. It hurts so badly when you can see something there in front of you; it seems so real; and to have to come to terms with the realization that it isn't and it is not part of reality at all. I do not think it is on the cards for us. We have been through so much over these three years. I am so fortunate to have met all these amazing people and I would do anything for Vitalab. The process didn't work for me and, let's be honest, I have been through many different simulations, processes, whatever you want to call it. They all just did not work. So, we are going to have to see the doctor on the 19th of January. I wanted to apologize for taking up all of his time. He has been nothing but understanding, loving, giving, generous in so many ways. Once we put the last three zygotes back, it will be the end and I will be leaving with nothing but love and appreciation for all they have done and tried to do for us.

Initially, I resented the process; didn't like the doctor and those working there. Now I am so glad I met them. They have done nothing but be patient, loving, caring and supportive towards me, towards us. I will be very sad that the process will come to an end but unfortunately, there is nothing more they can do for us. Right now, I want to just let it go. It is what it is and I can not change anything. Upsetting! Tragic! Hurtful! There is nothing I can do. We do not deserve this, but as I said before, it is now about appreciating what I have, loving what I have and doing what I can for those around me and just carrying on with my life. There is nothing else I can do. Jared has been amazing with this, he is so strong and supportive and he said that I am not alone and we have suffered a serious loss here and we will work through it together and whatever the next step is it doesn't matter, we will face it together. I truly appreciate what he said! I really appreciate him. He has been such a source of love, light and strength for me. I couldn't have got this far without him ...

It is one thing to keep trying to conceive via IVF and to feel the pain of it simply not working. It is another thing altogether to start everything from square one and then to have to wait while the person you love most in the world is literally turned upside down; goes through a far more invasive procedure; and struggles to breathe properly as she wakes up. All this and still no glimmer of a pregnancy.

But what you realize after you have tried everything you possibly can is that this is not just about becoming parents and having a child. This is about the two of us. It always was. How we love and support each other has always been our greatest strength and nothing has taken more out of us than this ordeal.

At this point we would have done just about anything for a positive result. I would have been over the moon to say that my beautiful wife was carrying our child, but it was just not to be. All I could do or say was to hold myself together and hold Mich. I had to hide my emotions and do what I could to keep her positive for our absolute last-ditch attempt.

I honestly believed that there was a chance, but it was as slim as they come. This is a journey that wears you down and doesn't let go. We had kept everything so private that we were literally the only things holding each other up. Our love and humor had kept us strong and now, more than ever since our first visit to Vitalab, Mich needed me to reiterate that whatever the future held for us would be faced together – hand in hand.

Meeting My Angel

You never know what challenges others are going through – so just be nice!

End Or Beginning?

It was one of the final appointments with Dr G and it did not go well at all. I walked in, he hugged me and asked how we are doing. I immediately said that I do not think that this is happening at all. I do not believe that I will ever be able to carry my own children. Those words constantly resound in my mind with the realization that I had just verbalized giving up on a dream that I have for so long tried to achieve. Shattered! just like that. We take dreams for granted. We do not realize that just like people, our dreams are so delicate, so beautifully pieced together as one. Within an instant, the dream that you have so carefully and vividly visualized, can shatter like a mirror. The fragments can never be pieced back together as before. The initial response was that Dr G needs a new uterus to work with. He did not want to say to me "you can not have children." He did it in the most dignified and sincerest way possible and I truly appreciate it more than he may ever know.

Arriving at this interim point in the process, it was now imperative to discuss the different options available to us moving forward. We had a choice of three paths –

adoption, choose a surrogate or acceptance and live with it. We definitely want kids, so I really do not believe acceptance is our answer. I felt that if we just went the acceptance route, we would merely be skirting issues and I preferred to still run with my dreams, even though we needed to get there in a different manner. As we got deeper into the conversation and insecurities came out, we were all eventually in tears. He knows me so well! So much better than I ever thought. He knows my background, my case, personality, what I – we – have been through, so intimately. He has been nothing but amazing. Even though we are coming to the end of our fertility journey, I do not foresee a close in our relationship any time soon. I never thought I would say it but I feel like we have a really amazing bond and it is something that I really want to keep alive and going. He has been such a 'mensch' to me. I could not wish for a better person, much less, doctor to look after me. As our appointment came to a close, we said goodbye, promised to call and let him know what happens after we see the counselor and of course plan for another chat with Dr G to move forward with our very last attempt.

Both my husband and I went directly to the bathroom to wash our faces and clean up because we looked like shit. My eyes and face were bright red from crying. All I wanted to do was go home and have a stiff drink. I couldn't though. I had to pick myself up, dust myself off, and head straight off to work. After work we were meant to meet people for dinner. Naturally I was upset, felt very down, defeated. Yes, we still have three eggs left. The question is what do we do with them? We could either put them back into me using IVF to remove some of the pain that I chose to endure. Or we could have an attempt at another ZIFT. We could also choose to put them into a surrogate who would carry a baby for us or leave the frozen eggs there until we decided on the way forward. There was a lot to consider. For now though, I am taking it each day at a time, step by step. It is just so much easier for me to keep it quiet and just keep going. I get weepy at certain times of the day. Usually when I am alone. Initially it was first thing in the morning. I am getting there slowly but surely, though.

After much questioning, discussing and soul searching, I feel a lot more prepared and confident in the decision we made moving forward. We looked at the facts surrounding surrogacy and we both agreed that it is not the way forward for us. All that is left for us to choose now is ADOPTION. Yes, something I truly never thought we would see ourselves get involved with at all! We will go the private adoption route and see if maybe there is a little angel waiting for us out there.

Right now, we need to move on and make some real tough decisions concerning our future. We are finishing the fertility treatment with Dr G and while this is happening, we are getting the ball rolling with the adoption agency. Apparently, legally it is not possible to get a baby younger than 3 months. If we get a boy, he will have to be Brissed, which can only be done once the adoption is finalized and under anesthetic. There are a fortune of questions regarding legalities and Jewish religious requirements. I am just completely exhausted. I am honestly just finished, defeated, flat, out. If this is the route that has been planned for us in order to save a little soul then we will do so.

We went to see Anne yesterday. I was unhappy and angry when sitting with her. All she could do was listen, understand what my requests were, she heard me and acknowledged everything that I was saying. I explained exactly what we decided and of course she understood completely, although we still needed clearance from Doctor G. She would give us some feedback within the week. Obviously, I was very upset after the meeting with Anne. This was the last transfer ever! Just let that sink in. Unfortunately, or fortunately I could not wallow in my state as I had work constraints and deadlines to follow through with.

Hopefully when we meet with the adoption specialist on Monday she will put my mind at ease. I do not feel happy about this. I know I should be though. I know I should be excited and overjoyed to begin this new process but it comes with a lot of baggage, sadness, anger, frustration and I do not know if I can handle it. The unknown is worrying me. I just know that to have a turn around time for possibly three years is just not fair.

It is a hard reality when you get to this stage of a fertility process and to be forced to fully comprehend that you just can not have children. Unfortunately, you have to be alright with that fact and move on from there, in any which way that you choose. It is very tough! Anne asked me how I was doing and I did not really answer. I kind of looked away in the other direction and all I really wanted to do was sit in a corner and cry till the end of time. Those caring, kind-hearted, amazing people will always have a very special place in my heart.

Jared and I are always full of smiles, light, understanding. However, the team at Vitalab know the sadness, they know how tough it is for us and I really appreciate the love and support. We have been through hell for four years and now it is coming to an end only to have to begin another lengthy process. Why? Am I not meant to be a parent? Am I not meant to have my own kids to love and cherish? What about Jared? Is he not meant to be a dad and have children he can love? What is also bothering me is what will people say? How will they react? I have been told on numerous occasions that I should not worry about that at all. It is what it is.

So Zoe will be our go to lady who will be dealing with our adoption. She seems nice. She doesn't seem to take nonsense very well and she basically told me to get an attitude adjustment. What?! Like seriously! So we were sitting down and explained a bit about what has been happening with the fertility process. I mentioned that the next step for us is to put the last three zygotes back and we know nothing will come of it. She immediately stopped me and said I have to change my thinking. It impacts the body and if I keep saying that it will not happen, then it may turn out to be a self-fulfilling prophecy.

It all just seems so unbelievable. It is so far from what I imagined and from what I believed would happen. And yet this is our reality now. It is just such a strange and unimaginable situation.I just cannot believe that this is the point we have come to. It is however amazing, that we have the relationship that we do. We have endured so much! It would really be nice if we just caught a break and were just given the blessing of being parents to our own biological children. I want the next transfer to be successful more than anything but I do not know what else we can possibly do to calm me, to assure me that all will be well. I have even reframed my thoughts around the ZIFT in order to psychologically not block anything.

So, currently I am feeling alright. I am trying to wrap my head around the fact that we will have to go through with an adoption. It is very difficult for me but I keep telling myself that my child is out there looking for me and we need help to find him or her as well and this is the only way. We are in fact saving a child from a life that possibly would not have been a good one at all. I am certain that the life we will provide will be one of unconditional love, happiness, success and positivity.

We are back in the fertility process for the very last time. Dr G scanned me and all was fine. He gave the nod that he was confident to go ahead with the ZIFT. We then went to see the coordinator to plan for the last part of the process. I was a bit relieved knowing everything went well with the scan, but I knew what was to come within the week. We were all waiting with bated breath.

To my absolute horror, I got a call a few days before the transfer that Doctor G has broken his ankle and has been booked off. He would not be able to perform the transfer. One of the other doctors I preferred would then have to do Neupogen and my ZIFT. So I freaked out a bit but not as much as I expected.

The week leading up to the last ZIFT went very quickly. I came out of theatre feeling sore but not like the previous procedure. I waved my one finger at my other half to let him know I was happy to see and hear he was there with me. It was time to wee and leave and all was going well. I was meant to be back in the next few days for stitches to be removed, which was again agony but I took it like a big girl and we went on our merry way. The nausea and headaches had begun and I was feeling worse than the previous ZIFT. I had been injecting as instructed and doing everything in my power throughout the entire process. Eventually, the Friday morning that I was meant to have my blood test I opted out. It was Passover that night. I knew if I took the test the family would pick up that I am upset and I really did not want to ruin the evening for everyone.

That morning I needed the bathroom before we set out to do the last bit of shopping and preparation. As usual, I had become very well acquainted with bathrooms during the fertility process. I decided to wee before leaving the house and to my horror, I found a brown discharge when I wiped. Oh shit! I have never got this before. I knew this could not be a good sign and I called my other half and immediately told him. We got in contact with the counselor, Anne and Doctor G. Two mentioned I should possibly reconsider taking the test, although they did not push because they knew how we felt and that it may make things very difficult if we did. The weekend was excruciating. The brown discharge began going red, which could have gone one of two ways, either pregnancy or as I suspected I was getting my period. The blood test could not have come soon enough. The only thing we could do was hope and pray that everything was alright.

Deep down I knew the result was not good but still I held onto the hope that something was different and that this time would be better. I thought maybe there was a G-d looking down on me, caring for me, loving me, wanting the very best for me. I was wrong, my angel is down here on earth right next to me constantly and he is the reason for me being.

D-day! One of the girls from Vitalab called to find out if Anne must call me for the results or if I am coming in. I knew it would be a better idea for her to call me because it would have been very difficult for everyone if we went through for results. Immediately, after saying hello to Anne, I said "this is not a positive result." Anne said she was just about to say it as well and she said how sorry she was. I just broke. It was truly a very difficult day for me. This is officially the end of the road at Vitalab and although I still feel very connected to everyone there, it will never be the same again for us. We are not patients anymore. Our file is officially closed! We are now in the great outdoors, on our own and unsupervised. Anne said if we need anything at all we must just call them. As usual she was really wonderful. The tears just streamed down my face! A dream that I have tried to achieve for so long has ended in such abrupt finality. Anne called Jared immediately and he called me and said how sorry she was. I was distraught. I really wished for more for him. After a while I calmed down a bit and went back to my laptop. Anne very kindly called me back again a little later to check on me. I will surely miss her kindness, love and care! Of course the pharmacy I was pumped with was done and I could stop taking them immediately. I mournfully removed my estrogen patch and looked at all the medication I would stop taking. Wow, what a mess! What a complete fuck up! To go four years and end up right where we began is just cruel in this situation. Of course we are far more knowledgeable about my body and what it can and cannot do. Woop dee do!

It still does not change the fact that I cannot have kids, I never will. We set out on this route to be able to have children and find the little souls that belong with us and here we are, with nothing to show for it, except for a bank balance that is not as healthy as it could have been. I do not blame anyone! It is no-one's fault at all. We are given one body. We have to look after it and this is the body you are stuck with for life and what you get is what you get. Just be thankful and accepting. Make it count. Push the limits if you dare.

The outcome was not the one we wanted... it was hurtful, cruel, terrible, ungodly, uncaring. We have to move on unfortunately. We have set out on a process and that was to have kids and we will, we just have to use a slightly different route to get there. Unfortunately, the route chosen for us is not an easy one and I truly hope that anyone who decides to go for fertility, understands completely what they are in for. You can't possibly understand at the beginning, but you have to do research and know what is going on. Mostly you have to trust your doctor and know that he is doing all he can for you and cares deeply for you and in some cases, more than you may know. We are privileged to have the bond that we do with Doctor G. I cannot help feeling that although we have reached the end of the road at Vitalab, we will still have a very strong and ongoing connection with the organization and most of all with all the staff members there. They are the most wonderful people and I could not have wished for a better team to get to know and work on me. I just wish we would have had a different outcome and that the ending didn't come so quickly and so abruptly. I do however know that when one door closes, another one swings open. I just wish it did not work out this way and that the situation was different. Right now, each time I think of what has taken place, my eyes begin to fill with tears and I cannot help thinking, "forever in our hearts." I will treasure them forever and will try and remember the past four years as best as I can. Whatever comes our way I hope I will be able to welcome it with open arms and that the bond between us and our future kids will be that much deeper! I do not know what will happen, which is frustrating. However, I cannot help thinking that maybe we will have a little surprise sooner than it will take for me to have my own child.

For the moment, my emotions are raw. I am bereaved, deeply saddened. For whatever reason I am not meant to carry my own children and it is not for me to control or question. There are parts of my body that are not working the way it should and it is not my fault. It is nobody's fault. We can only hope for a brighter and happier tomorrow. Because of the process we went though at Vitalab, our relationship became stronger and far better than it has ever been. I will always be very thankful for this!

A new chapter of our lives must begin now and I just hope it is quick and filled with joy, health, success and lots of happiness. What we have been through, I would not wish on my worst enemy! What we have been through has been terribly cruel and so much more painful than anyone can imagine. I do not know why this has all happened to us. I guess we just need to continue as a strong united couple and we will achieve anything together!

After all these years, having to take time out of our schedule, going to Vitalab for scans, counseling, seeing doctors, being on medication, ups, downs, looking at screens, being injected, getting blood taken, needles, stitches, scheduled doctors appointments and so much more, it is suddenly all over. Just like that my life is now one big question mark and although I know the direction that we are going in, I just do not understand why we landed up in this position. Unfortunately, there are some questions that we simply have no answer to ...

There are people who come into our lives and profoundly influence them. They may be a parent, a friend, an acquaintance or something altogether different. They may come into our lives for a brief period, years or always be there. I have always believed that everyone we meet is there for a reason, obvious or not. The team at Vitalab were always meant to be a part of our lives but not in the obvious way.

When we started our journey there, we thought it would be a situation of getting pregnant with the help of doctors, nurses and some pretty talented embryologists. We never expected to build the relationships we did where we would laugh and cry together and just be able to pick up the phone to find out how they are doing. I guess we just didn't expect to leave with a whole second family. Dr G, Anne, Lynne, Calista, Colleen..... everyone should be as lucky and experience the unconditional support we have from such special people.

The journey had just taken a whole new shape and despite everything the trajectory felt like a boomerang that was hurtling back at us. Everything felt like we were starting from scratch. Adoption was now our only option that we were prepared to take if we were to be parents. I felt completely vulnerable. I knew precious little about the process, where to start or who to even get help from.

And then came Zoe....

Meeting My Angel

You never know what challenges others are going through – so just be nice!

Forever In Our Hearts

As one process ends and another begins, it was terribly difficult to comprehend what had just taken place. What we went through for those four years in fertility treatment, as well as on our own, was immensely painful but at the same time, exceptionally rewarding in so many ways. Although the process itself did not assist us in falling pregnant, it gave us so much more as a couple and a necessary push to be able to start finding our little angel down here on earth. Before our fertility journey began, in the back of my mind, I somehow knew that the treatments would not work. However, I wanted to prove myself wrong. I really wanted to explore all the avenues, medically and alternatively, if there were any, to see if I could fall pregnant. I so desperately wanted to be wrong! Looking back, although we went through hell, I would give anything to be able to do it again. However, the lessons learned through the process, although heartbreaking, were so rewarding. To be able to trust oneself is immeasurably important. It may hurt at times and it may be very difficult and to trust one's own thoughts, but if you push past the emotion and the possibility that it is terrifying then there is so much that you have to gain. Creating that bond with oneself, trusting and loving oneself is one of the most imperative things in life. Although, lets not forget that at times we do not want to let certain opportunities and situations pass us by, which can only be achieved if we do not listen to that little voice inside of us.

After the treatments ended and we got the last call from Vitalab, I decided to dedicate a poem to those little angels that we did not and will not ever get to meet. Coming to terms with the fact that I cannot provide my other half with children was a very difficult realization. However, it showed me that my inner strength, resilience and love far surpasses anything I ever had to deal with. I am grateful for where I am today, for what we as a couple have managed to achieve and it would not have been possible without the constant love, support and compassion from Jared and those few people who knew what was actually going on.

As for those beautiful little angelic souls that we never met and will never meet. I am sorry. I would have loved for you to have been mine, ours. Sadly, there were other plans in the wings that were made for us. I can only wish that some day you will be received as a gift by a very lucky set of parents who will love and cherish every second with you. You are so loved and will always be remembered even though our connection was made so brief. May your souls live on forever and that you only know love!

Forever In Our Hearts

You were so little. So precious, a gift from above that I never knew existed. A gift that sadly would never be a reality for him or me.

As I lay on the table waiting for the doctor to insert you into me so I could give life to you, my heart pounding, mixed feelings like a roller coaster of emotions, up, down, nausea, headaches. Just calm down he tells me, relax everything is fine.

Seven times we tried and seven times we failed. Eventually came the words "I wish it would just end!"

But so abruptly, those days are now gone. Days filled with worry, pain, sickness, are all gone. What I would do to have it all again and again and again. This song that you have left in my heart will forever remain.

Sadly we now must part ways and continue our journey of many empty days. Empty, because you are not with me, empty because you are lost to me. I must now roam this earth, looking for a child who has been given up at birth. Left by parents who cannot manage to hold its worth.

The honor will be mine. You will see again the sun will shine, brighter than before. It will be filled with love, laughter and success that this family has never known before. I only wish we got the chance to know you, meet you, hold your gorgeous little hands, kiss those small precious toes. Dry your eyes from tears when you bump yourself or hurt your nose. How I wish you were with us now growing, healthy, loving, having fun.

Our time was cut short and this memory will I cherish and hold forever, for forever in my heart you will remain. Lives of the unborn we never got to physically meet and greet but spiritually, you were such a treat.

Your smell, your clothes, I can feel, see, hear and smell you. I feel so close to you, but why can't we meet you? So abruptly you were swept away, to never be known on a special day.

I will fondly and sadly savor your precious little souls and forever I wish you were the one I could hold. To love you and laugh with you, get you ready for school, brush your hair and teeth and give you food.

I should just resign myself to the fact that not all of us are privileged and given that which can be given only by Heaven. Alas we have tried and nothing has been brought so continue we shall no matter how distraught. Dark, stormy, angry tears for someone above who doesn't care to hear. My angels above, I wish one thing for you that someone so deserving can receive the gift of you. A gift you shall be but not for us as our bond was not meant to be in this world filled with tumultuous disgust.

As I close this door of suffering, agony and more, I fondly remember the laughter, love and how we have been adored. Forever in my heart you will always remain I hope not as wound but as a memory filled with love, not pain. How hard it has been to say goodbye and I wonder what to do with the medication as each day goes by. You were my only hope and I am thankful for you for forever in my heart I shall keep you too. My father in a million how sorry I am that this did not work we tried every conceivable plan! But continue we must with heads held high and remember the memory of the kids who secretly died. Is this really the word to use, I am not sure but use it I will because it is what I feel- it's so pure. I am sorry all this is it now, forward we must go, I am not sure how.

A lady awaits us and the process is there filled with paperwork and pen-pushers and legalities to scare. But ahead we will push together as a team and love one another for we will achieve our dream. We must believe! Please do! I need you to do it with me for I feel lost without you. Let's continue this journey and see where we go, in love and light we unfortunately have to let them go.

Love and leave you my precious children we must, for your earth parents will be waiting for you in the physical to give you all that you trust. We will be here waiting and ready we shall be to receive you as a delivery, as a gift to him and me.

No words!! Just devastated, distraught, shattered – for Mich; for me; for us! I have read Mich's poetry before, but none cut as deep as this one. All I could think was "Why not us???!!!"

Meeting My Angel

You never know what challenges others are going through – so just be nice!

Turning Over A New Leaf

A rejuvenating and uplifting holiday was so needed! We basically flipped a coin between Israel and Mauritius. In all the years we had been together we had never visited Israel as a couple. However, Mauritius was a very special place for us because – well – that was where we went on our honeymoon. We decided to choose Israel and we were so happy that we did because it really gave us the healing that we needed after all we had been through.

From the moment we got off the plane we did not stop for a second! It was amazing to see the family. As always they were just phenomenal. Each place we visited was better than the next and we were so grateful that we could not only be with family and connect with them but also have the time to be together that we so desperately needed – and of course – we had time to heal. The feeling of security, love, appreciation, acceptance was palpable throughout our stay. However, this holiday also allowed me the opportunity to sit back and decide what I wanted in life moving forward; where we would be going now; and of course what it was that we would be needing. During the fertility treatment, you are so focused on getting through each cycle; getting through that scan; saving as much money as is humanly possible for the little person who will be entering both your lives. We simply just forget to live! We may not necessarily neglect ourselves, however we somehow forget to truly enjoy living, being with one another, just sleeping together for pure pleasure rather than procreation. We forget to just be!

We got home from our holiday and I was sitting in my office and I realized just how quiet it was. It was a silence that I knew needed to be filled with excited screeches and laughter that only babies can bring. "Nothing will happen if I do not make it!" As these words resounded in my mind, I called Jared and we decided that it was best to move forward with the adoption process, as daunting as it was. I gave Zoe a call and within a week or so we had our first home visit. I thought it would be far more invasive and stressful. Zoe was very calm, informative and relaxed. The visit went very well and we then had to complete a huge list of items to get going with the adoption process. Within three or so weeks we had completed everything on that form that we could. We also made an appointment to have a psychological evaluation, which was a requirement for the process. We created a profile for the birth parents, as now we had to sell ourselves and hope that we would be chosen as adoptive parents to a beautiful little boy or girl. It just never ends! ...

How do you eat an elephant? One bite at a time. How do you go about adopting a baby? One step at a time. There are just a heck of a lot of them. Couple that together with some absolutely amazing people; some insane bureaucratic hurdles; a need for ton-loads of fortitude and an iron will.

Israel was an amazing turning point for us. We got the opportunity to let ourselves relax and just enjoy where we were and, more importantly, each other. Getting away from everything helped us let go of a great deal of the pain we had been through. We realized that we had just not given ourselves a chance to just be. And we needed it. What followed was a whirlwind. Who would have thought that endurance was a prerequisite for becoming a parent but if there was one thing we had learned to do over the last 4 ½ years it was to endure.

Meeting My Angel

You never know what challenges others are going through – so just be nice!

And We Still Go Marching On!

When we got back from our whirlwind trip, I sat in my office and looked at all the medication that I had been taking and was left over. Of course, I was never going to need them again. I thought for a little while and eventually when I finally came to terms with what was taking place, I decided that it may be a good idea for me to take a trip to Vitalab and donate the leftover medication to a deserving couple trying to conceive, who were unable to afford it. Every little bit helps along the way, whether big or small. I handed the packet to Anne and gave her instructions and after getting big hugs and lots of love from the staff members, I left feeling light, exceptionally happy, proud. I had given with an open heart and with a wish that the medication would have a positive impact and assist in a couple conceiving.

As each day passed and the more I felt a sense of giving and helping others, the dark period seemed to slowly subside. I was then jolted back into my reality when I remembered that I had to get on with preparation for the adoption. Within the adoption process you are told to make sure your network is as large as possible. You never know who might know of someone who is wanting to give up a baby. Funnily enough, there was someone in our network that we had no idea would be able to assist. We were referred on to a friend of hers, based in KZN, who was also an adoption social worker. Zoe got in touch and handled everything for us as there was a baby that was due to be born in June. As a couple you are not allowed to get involved with anything concerning a child. You are actually not meant to even know that a child might be waiting in the wings, because if the adoption does not materialize then the opportunity for disappointment is that much greater.

So late in June I was sitting at around five pm in the Sandton area, waiting patiently for a client to arrive from work and begin our session, minding my own business. I then get a call from a very emotional Jared saying that there is a baby with our name on it. At this stage we did not have all of the information, however we were told later that the father was expectant of certain things, which seemed unreasonable and not according to the process and legalities that we knew of. I listened carefully and immediately I got a feeling that there was something very wrong with this fit.

Weeks passed, the baby was due to be born. We had been keeping in touch with Zoe as we were supposed to do. After each call we received through the social worker, the story became more absurd and it felt like this was not what was wanted going into something so beautiful. Eventually, I had a little chateroo with my other half and we both thought it was a good idea to just let this opportunity go. Previously, we had both told the social worker that this did not feel right and we were not happy with the fit and she always replied that she did not want to take this possible opportunity away from us.

Eventually I had enough of the entire situation and I said that I did not want this for the family. It was not the right fit at all. I did not care if we had to wait forever, but this was something that just felt wrong. With this response, we got news of a possible baby to be born in the near future and that we should keep in touch, however we also had to allow the social worker to do her job.

Of course, finding out that there was a good chance that we could very soon be parents, naturally we decided to do a bit of research. Our Sundays, and every other opportunity we had, were consumed by running to and from different baby shops. If a shop was open in the evenings as well, we went there. When parents to be are in the pregnancy phase, there is a nine or eight month period where you have the opportunity to think, prepare for the little one, plan. The adoption process is vastly different in that you become a parent literally overnight! You blink and poof there it is! So, obviously, in between everything else, you have to make the time to do your research, pick names, plan a room, I don't know – maybe even buy a cot. You never know when a baby might just sneak up on you ...

Who would have thought that our story would read like an international thriller? The possibility of a baby turned into an attempt at extortion by the baby's father who we had never met; a mother who none of the social workers had ever seen and us deciding to walk away from what was an ugly situation. We wanted everything to be right. Naïve? Possibly Idealistic? Probably! But we did not want negativity to overshadow everything. We had been through so much already and if there is one thing you need to avoid, it is any form of negativity.

So we decided to do exactly what expectant parents do.

We focused on the positive. We believed ...

Meeting My Angel

You never know what challenges others are going through – so just be nice!

Light At The End Of The Tunnel

Turning down the possibility of having a complete family in the future is certainly something that needed a lot of consideration and soul searching. However, the decision to turn the baby down in KZN felt right for many reasons. The words "I do not want this for the family, this feels wrong. I do not care if we have to wait forever." that so clearly resounded in my mind, provided such a relief. It was as if I had completely let go of the desperation and I was once again able to think clearly, rationally about something that would have a major impact in the future on us as a couple as well as for the family as a whole.

I had been so focused on how I was going to explain that we were prepared to wait for eternity until the right angel found us, that I did not prepare myself for the words that there is a possible baby waiting with our name on it. There was a sense of calm that came over me. A feeling that for once in such a long time, everything in the world is right now. Everything is working in our favor and in the way that it should be. I did not get emotional about it. I listened, I took everything in and I realized that now we have to wait patiently. Shit! Patience is certainly not one of my virtues, however adoption is a waiting game. Just knowing that this was a beautiful opportunity coming our way, gave me a renewed sense that there are definitely angels watching out for us and are working tirelessly to make sure we hear them and follow the path that has been set out for us.

We spent the next few months tirelessly running around doing the research needed for our newcomer. Although we did not have all the information we needed, we managed to get a very good idea of what products are out there, which ones are decent to use, as well as those which are not at all good. Eventually, the end of November arrived. We were offered tickets to attend Mama Magic – the Baby Expo and we decided to take the opportunity to go and look around. We decided that even if this little angel does not come home to us, we still needed to see the products and learn a little bit more. Of course I did not know what to do because our little angel had become adoptable. However, we had not met him yet. To buy a pram, car seat and a few other items and not meet our baby was very daunting. We were told to rather take a bit of money with and ask the people if we could reserve items and once we were happy after meeting the baby, we could pay in full and accept delivery of the items. This worked out a little differently.

We spoke with a very accommodating lady, who said that she would take the items back if anything went wrong with the adoption. We just needed to pay in full and if there was an issue, she was happy to take the knock herself. I was so overwhelmed that I walked in and out of the bedroom with the items the whole weekend as I could not believe that we had just paid for a pram and carseat for a baby that we have not even met yet. The only question I could ask Jared was "are you sure?" The response I received was "I have never been more sure about anything!"

By Monday afternoon, in the first week of December 2018, Zoe came to fetch me to meet our new little angel. She asked if my "heart was going boom, boom, boom?" I did not initially understand her and responded that I was perfectly alright and there was no pounding. As I got out of the car and we began walking up the stairs into the home, my chest started beating fast; my thoughts needed collecting. There it is. I understand what she now means. We met our little angel and named him Raphael. The name we chose comes from the Angel of Healing. He is the most gorgeous, loving, precocious, little angel that we have ever set our eyes on. From the moment I held him in my arms for the first time, I only heard my mind saying "buddy you are coming home!" Love at first sight was a definite! Those gorgeous blue eyes captivated me like nothing before and I could not have imagined the first meeting to be anything like this. I never imagined that we would ever adopt, although I knew from the start of our journey that there was a twist in the tale.

Our little angel is now living happily with us. Each and every day is filled with love, laughter, excitement, song! A deep void has been filled and we are so thankful that we have been blessed with our angel. We ask that our journey can be shared with as many people as possible and that those out there who are struggling and going through dark periods do not feel so alone. The darkness eventually subsides, it can not last forever. You have to want to see the light though and not every situation must be dealt with in an emotional manner. Life is full of curve balls, which unfortunately, or fortunately, we have no control over. Keep going, keep hoping, keep loving! Everything works out as it always should. We may not like the plan; we may not like the way in which it happens or even turns out, but there is always a path that is set out for us and we just need to stay on it and keep moving. Within an instant our lives changed for the better, we became new parents overnight and every moment is treasured. Although, we do have our moments, as families do, we are thankful and strive to be the very best parents that this little angel could ever have or even hope for! Thank you for reading! Thank you for caring and for taking an interest in our journey. We wish that what you are going through does not make you feel alone and in the dark. There is always someone to talk to, there is always someone there thinking of you and loving you!

Keep going! keep hoping! Keep loving! xxx ...

The whirlwind continued but this time it was different. This time we had our son on the way. Only one time before in my life had anything felt this right. And it felt that much more special.

Along the way we had doubted ourselves and each other. We had lost trust in the world and regained it. Our love for each other grew and our journey that led us to Raphy gave me my wife back. Mich was intensely private and untrusting while we were going through IVF after IVF. She completely came out of her shell during the adoption process. She is the coolest and most loving mom and soulmate.

How do you get to your happy ending? Love without boundaries. Give each other space to heal. Learn to let go of the pain. Embrace the blessings that come your way in their own time. And I always remember the words of Master Oogway from Kung Fu Panda:

"Yesterday is History

Tomorrow is a Mystery

But Today is a Gift

That is why it is called The Present"

I live every day grateful for my gifts, my two angels, Michelle and Raphy.

And Then The Healing Began

Our journey in finding Raphy and becoming parents has been nothing short of a rollercoaster – and Mich did a far better job than I ever could to get that across. But now it is my turn to share part of our incredible journey. For those of you who have been following the blog, I have been referred to as Mich's other half, her Jared, but two titles make me prouder and happier than any others – the love of Mich's life and Raphy's daddy. It is really simple why. They are the loves of my life!

We always knew we were going to have a rough time conceiving children but there was never a doubt in my mind who I wanted to spend the rest of my life with; moan to; annoy with endless useless facts; have put up with my man flu (it is a real thing!); and share the joys of parenthood with. We tried naturally. We tried unnaturally. We tried just about anything and clung to hope to carry us through each disappointment.

Well, disappointment is a complete and utter understatement – each negative result was devastating. Our hearts were ripped out of our chests and then pieced back together by our extended family at Vitalab; hope that a miracle would happen and our love for each other. No-one else really knew what we were going through. And if they did, we didn't share every thought or emotion with them. It was just too painful.

The rest of the story you know. You may have even shared a lot of our emotions – heartbreak and joy. Our worlds have changed immeasurably and the best way I can think of sharing how much it has changed is how we chose our little angel's name.

We chose his second name first. It actually chose him. We quite literally started talking about names, and knowing that the process had been just as much spiritual, as physical, for us, we decided that his second name would be Elad. Loosely this means G-D is eternal. There was always a sense that whatever we were going through was decided already and we were just "along for the ride." That was the easy part!

Finding the name that everyone would call him was far more challenging – or so we thought.

It was only when we first met Raphy, and realised what he meant to us – and would mean to everyone else – that we decided on his name, Raphael (Healer of G-d). This tiny little angel had started healing our broken hearts from the moment we saw him – and at 14 months he continues to live up to his name, bringing joy and love wherever he goes.

Before Raphy, Mich and I had become stressed, irritable and angry. Almost everything was a burden; a competition; a battle. This was never how we were before. We were always positive and enjoyed life but this gradually became more and more difficult to bear with each failed IVF. Each one felt like we had lost a child. By the time the last ZIFT took place we had been in mourning for 4 ½ years. But we had each other and we were going to make sure that we grew our family. We had wanted this for so long.

We had two options. The first was surrogacy. The second adoption. In our hearts, though, there was only ever one option. And so we started the adoption process. We were warned about how administrative the process would be and that there were never any guarantees when or if we would find a child for us to love. So we got the ball rolling – and then went to Israel.

It was the most special holiday we had ever been on – not just because of where we went – but because we were together. We even got soaked in a flooding rain together. Before we would have been angry and found anything else to be worried about. We just rolled with it – and looked like two drowned rats in the process. We literally soaked in everything we could!

Back to reality, we got to work gathering the evidence for the adoption that we are not sex offenders, criminals, psychologically scarred (maybe a little strange) or medically unfit. We were counseled, went to an adoption group and put together a profile of ourselves that was hopefully going to convince complete strangers to choose Mich and me as the adoptive parents of a child that we did not even know yet. Reality hit hard when we were exposed to how cruel, callous and desperate people can be. Here we were, prepared to do everything within our power (legally) to become parents and we heard of a couple that were having their eighth child and ended up selling him!!! How could anyone take life for granted like this? How could anyone be so abusive? And then we got the news that there was a certain little "Shpoonk" (as Mich likes to call Raphy) that was meant for us – a little angel that we had been waiting to meet for so long.

We got to meet Raphy for the first time on the 3rd of December, just short of ten months after we started the adoption process. I guess we just had a very long "overdue pregnancy". And then on the 19th of December, after sitting in front of a magistrate for what seemed like an absolute age, with a sleeping 5-month old draped over Mich's chest Raphy came home ...

www.ingramcontent.com/pod-product-compliance
Ingram Content Group UK Ltd.
Pitfield, Milton Keynes, MK11 3LW, UK
UKHW020417250726
13967UKWH00007B/2685

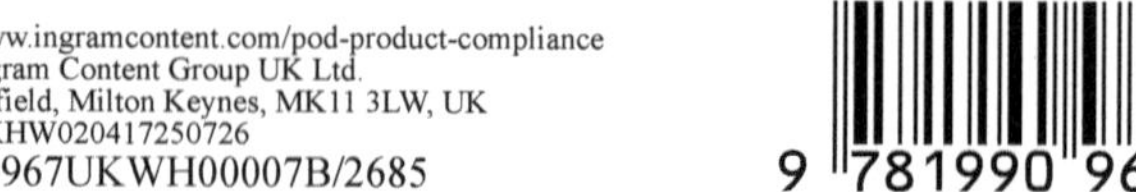